I recently completed the reading of *The Fight Is Already Fixed*. It is a powerhouse of scriptural encouragement for Christians who may be dealing with struggles and wonder how they can be victorious in their Spiritual lives. I have been in the ministry for 47 years, and have read many books of this kind, but *The Fight Is Already Fixed* clearly pictures the reality of our actual combat against our adversary. The Author (with whom I am personally acquainted) has a history of being a professional boxer, a military person who has seen the field of battle, and is a strong Christian who has faced numerous struggles in his spiritual life. This book is a personal portrait of his own life laid out there to be an encouragement for others. You will never be sorry that you have taken the time to read this book.

—Chaplain Bob Anders, LTC, USAF (Ret)

THE FIGHT
IS ALREADY FIXED

MARK LANTON
Presents

THE FIGHT
IS ALREADY FIXED
THIS *12 Round* FIGHT WE CALL LIFE

"And the devil, who deceived them, was thrown into the lake of burning sulfur, where the beast and the false prophet had been thrown.
They will be tormented day and night for ever and ever."

REVELATION 20:10

TATE PUBLISHING & *Enterprises*

Published by Tate Publishing & Enterprises, LLC
127 E. Trade Center Terrace | Mustang, Oklahoma 73064 USA
1.888.361.9473 | www.tatepublishing.com

Tate Publishing is committed to excellence in the publishing industry. The company reflects the philosophy established by the founders, based on Psalm 68:11,
"The Lord gave the word and great was the company of those who published it."

Book design copyright © 2009 by Tate Publishing, LLC. All rights reserved.
Cover design by Kandi Evans
Interior design by Stefanie Rooney

Published in the United States of America

ISBN: 978-1-60799-453-4
1. Religious, Christian 2. Application
11.03.25

ACKNOWLEDGMENTS

I first want to thank my Lord and Savior Jesus Christ for this vision to worship him via this book. I could have been dead or in prison, but God's grace has smiled on me for no apparent reason. I could have been addicted to drugs and alcohol or engaged in a life of crime. I am not worthy of his love, but he loves me anyway. I am honored to kneel at his feet and acknowledge him as my creator.

I also want to thank all of the Christian warriors I befriended at Balad Air Base, Iraq. I pray all these good people are blessed and they continue to run that race that God has designated for their lives. You all have played a significant role in my spiritual growth, and I certainly appreciate your friendship.

I want to thank the 332nd Expeditionary Aerospace Medicine Squadron, AEF 3/4 2008, Joint Base Balad, Iraq, where I was superintendent. I had an awesome group to serve with.

The church I was raised in, St. John's Deliverance Tabernacle in Nyack, New York, where my mother got saved when she was pregnant with me. I thank God for blessing me with Johanna Lee Lanton as my mother.

My pastor, Dr. Bernard C. Yates, who has continued to inspire me over the years. You promoted my spirit to look beyond any limits, and this book is a result of your encouragement and influence.

My nephew, Louis E. Lanton II, who is my spiritual "booster." Thank you for the motivation.

Last but not least, I want to thank those individuals who took pleasure to know of any hardship and difficulties that I have encountered. I want to acknowledge all those folks who embodied gossip to spread on my behalf and yet smiled in my presence. I have the impetus to recognize those who were determined to discredit my name and "diss" me out of envy, jealousy, and discontent. Satan infiltrated your hearts and exploited you as my stumbling block, but God has turned you all into my stepping stones. I thank God for the strength to "stay on the wall" (reference Round 7). I publicly forgive you, and I pray for your lives to be blessed.

TABLE OF CONTENTS

PRE-FIGHT WARMUP

Revelation 20:10 (NIV) states, "And the devil, who deceived them, was thrown into the lake of burning sulfur, where the beast and the false prophet had been thrown. They will be tormented day and night for ever and ever." This book is based on the above verse, proving *the fight is already fixed.* We invite you to join Mark A. Lanton in this sensational twelve-round championship boxing match commentary, turning the fight scenarios into the analogy of a Christian walk. This book will illustrate the situations a boxer encounters during a boxing match and make the parallel to life issues we face as Christians. These writings are intended to provide encouragement and strength in *this twelve-round fight we call life.* The above verse is referenced to the sport of boxing because of the author's extensive background as a former military (all-army/armed-forces) boxing champion and a former professional boxer. It makes it an easy illustration for the author to define, making it entertaining, educational, and inspiring. As this single verse is referenced to a boxing match, it verifies that our spiritual fight is already pre-destined. We already know who is going to win this spiritual fight. It doesn't matter how battered we get in our earthly life. It doesn't matter the amount of abuse we receive, we know that victory belongs to those who are in Christ. The author attained the idea for this book in the middle of the night in a vision during a combat deployment in the desert of Iraq, the birthplace of Abraham, where he first received the Word of God.

Whether you're a teenager or you're ninety years old, it is never too late or too early to accept Christ as your personal Savior. *This twelve-round fight we call life* does not start until you are saved. Up until the point of you getting saved, your name is not written in the Book of Life (eternal life). Revelations 20:15 (NIV) plainly says, "If anyone's name was not found written in the book of life, he was thrown into the lake of fire." This means you have fallen short of the mighty hand of God and your eternal destination is the pit of hell. The Book of Life is a list of names of who will live with God forever in heaven.

Deciding on your career path or who you will marry are very important life decisions, but your salvation is the most important decision you will ever make.

This book is intended to serve as an encouragement to you in your walk in the Lord, and inspire those who are struggling in their faith. The Bible clearly states in Hebrews 11:6 (NIV), "And without faith it is impossible to please God, because anyone who comes to him must believe that he exists and that he rewards those who earnestly seek him." Developing faith does not always happen instantaneously. You must work your way in to the realm of bearing true faith. Hebrews 11:1 (NIV) distinguishes the elements of faith: "Now faith is being sure of what we hope for and certain of what we do not see."

The sport of boxing is extremely violent in nature. The goal of boxing is to inflict physical damage upon your opponent. As Christians, our spiritual boxing match is also violent. It says in Matthew 11:12 (NIV), "From the days of John the Baptist until now, the kingdom of heaven has been forcefully advancing, and forceful men lay hold of it." We must constantly keep our spiritual guard up. Through this book, you will read many analogies on how the perfect word of God refers to a boxer in the midst of a twelve-round match. These comparisons will illustrate the wonder of our Lord and Savior Jesus Christ, and bring an understanding to the importance of our salvation.

THE CONVERSION

This twelve-round fight we call life does not begin until you accept Jesus Christ as your Lord and personal Savior. Up until this point in your life, you are destined for eternal damnation. The Bible says in Romans 6:23 (NIV), "For the wages of sin is death, but the gift of God is eternal life in Christ Jesus our Lord."

Being a "good" person is not enough to get you into heaven. Paying your taxes, volunteering, helping the poor, or being president of your local PTA is not adequate to be in the presence of our heavenly Father. In fact, being a church member isn't going to give you the access to eternal life. There are many churchgoers who have occupied pews Sunday after Sunday for countless years. Many are involved with various church activities, such as Sunday school teachers, ushers, ministers, and even pastors. These are all wonderful functions within the body of Christ, but God requires your belief and faith in our king of the universe, Jesus Christ.

John 3:16 (NIV) simply states, "For God so loved the world that he gave his one and only Son that whoever believes in him shall not perish but have eternal life." This is the key to infinite life. Believing with all your heart the above verse to be true, your life is brand new. You are a born-again child of the living God. Just like a newborn child, new believers need to be nourished and fed the *Word of God* so that they may gain strength and knowledge to resist and overcome the attacks of Satan. Being saved does not mean you will not make mistakes, nor does it mean you will not have troubles. It says you now have the source that can forgive you, and a means to develop your life into the creature you were designed to be. *This twelve-round fight we call life* has just begun the moment you accept Christ.

As a boxer prepares for a fight, he will study his opponent in many different ways. He reviews tapes of the opponent's past fights to see what they are vulnerable to. He looks at how his opponent throws punches, and he assesses their strength. As he studies his opponent, he can also determine the opponent's level of passion to win. Many times, a boxing match is not determined by the skills and abilities of the athletes; it is resolved by who has the stronger diligence to win. Hebrews 6:11 (NIV) states, "We want each of you to show this same diligence to the very end, in order to make your hope sure." There are some fighters who only fight hard up until the point they get tired. When fatigue sets in, they lose that hunger to win.

This is a spiritual warfare, and you will encounter the enemy for the rest of your natural life. In addition to the spiritual war I am fighting as a Christian, I am currently serving my second tour as a combat medic in the Iraq War. I believe it was meant for me to write this book in this environment. God plucked me out of my comfortable home and my luxury cars, and literally separated me from my comfortable life and home. He placed me in the barren desert of Babylon (literally). The triple-digit heat on a daily basis was a minor inconvenience compared to the barrages of mortar rockets that came our direction on a regular basis. As a medic, I administered medical care to the wounded soldiers, sailors, airmen, and marines every day. The devastating injuries I saw and treated were traumatic to the point where I did not want to see another double-amputee or an open-head injury. The images of these warriors who were laid up in traction and connected to ventilators broke my heart. Through all that I witnessed and experienced, I certainly became stronger in my faith because I know many of these heroes should be dead as a result of their wounds, but God spared their lives. God has reasons for bringing people into certain circumstances. I may not know the reasons, but I trust it is all part of his perfect plan, because God knows everything about anything. Acts 15:18 (NIV) says, "... that have been known for ages." It also says in 1 John 3:20 (NIV), "Whenever our hearts condemn us. For God is greater than our hearts, and he knows everything."

I often reflected as I treated these wounded warriors, that I could be lying on that stretcher connected to a chest tube and ventilator. But God saw fit to show his mercy on me. The Bible says in Psalm 91:7 (NIV), "A thousand may fall at your side, ten thousand at your right hand, but it will not come near you."

The mortar rockets exploded all around me, and it hit others, but it did not touch me. I thank God for the covering, and I will always pray for my fellow wounded warriors.

Now that our fighter has studied our opponent and he knows their normal method of operation in the ring, it's time to prepare for the fight. For the Christian, your spiritual opponent is not the typical fighter with average abilities and predictable moves. Your spiritual opponent can adapt to any style of fighting you present. Your spiritual opponent is lightning fast with knock-out power in either hand. For *this twelve-round fight we call life,* your spiritual opponent is Satan.

Immediately prior to the beginning of any boxing match, the fighters step to the middle of the ring and receive instructions from the referee. At the end of the instructions, the referee always says, "Protect yourselves at all times."

For the Christian, a child of our heavenly Father, protecting yourselves at all times means that you must wear your whole armor of God at all times until the end. Ephesians 6:11–17 (NIV) states:

> "Put on the full armor of God so that you can take your stand against the devil's schemes. For our struggle is not against flesh and blood, but against the rulers, against the authorities, against the powers of this dark world and against the spiritual forces of evil in the heavenly realms. Therefore put on the full armor of God, so that when the day of evil comes, you may be able to stand your ground, and after you have done everything, to stand. Stand firm then, with the belt of truth buckled around your waist, with the breastplate of righteousness in place, and with your feet fitted with the readiness that comes from the gospel of peace. In addition to all this, take up the shield of faith, with which you can extinguish all the flaming arrows of the evil one. Take the helmet of salvation and the sword of the Spirit, which is the word of God."

This is the only way for us to protect ourselves at all times:

Immediately prior to the start of the boxing

match, our fighter gets down on his knees in his corner and says a prayer. By saying a prayer for everyone to witness, our fighter has shown not to be ashamed to acknowledge God in the presence of others. Matthew 11:6 (NIV) says, "Blessed is the man who does not fall away on account of me." I exhort for you not to be embarrassed or ashamed to acknowledge God in places other than church. Those who witness your acknowledgment of God will see your example and may be encouraged by the boldness in your worship.

The bell rings, and the fight has begun. The arena is full of spectators, cheering for both fighters. In your typical boxing match, there are three judges. These judges watch for punches scored, ring generalship, and aggressiveness. For the Christian in *this twelve-round fight we call life*, there are also three judges. The *Son*, *Father*, and *Holy Spirit*, and they are all as one. He is sitting on a throne in heaven. His name is Jesus Christ. He is watching every round of your life while you are spiritually boxing against Satan.

Normally, in the first round of a boxing match, a fighter is full of energy. They are fresh, with quick reflexes and a high level of confidence. Philippians 1:6 (NIV) states, "Being confident of this, that he who began a good work in you will carry it on to completion until the day of Christ Jesus." As long as you stick with the plan of living obedient, you are sure to be victorious. The plan of action for obtaining victory in this spiritual fight are the Holy Scriptures. You're a new believer, and you are feeling like you are standing on top the world.

In our fighter's enthusiasm and energy, he comes out swinging with lefts and rights to the head of our opponent. His attack is somewhat effective, but our opponent sits and lurks for him to drop his guard. For Christians, the serpent is lurking for you to get careless so he can capitalize, and set you up with the counter punches of sin. Numbers 33:11 (NIV) states, "They left the Red Sea and camped in the Desert of Sin." This Scripture refers to the Israelites and how they complained to Moses because they didn't have any food or water in the desert wilderness. The purpose was for Moses to lead his people out of the hand of bondage and into the land of milk and honey. The people he led began to object and criticize Moses for bringing them to the wilderness without the basic necessities. They had lost focus on who their ultimate provider was, and it was not Moses, it was the Lord. Moses said to them in Exodus 17:2 (NIV), "So they quarreled with Moses and said, 'Give us water to drink.' Moses replied, 'Why do you quarrel with me? Why do you put the LORD to the test?'" This is one method where Satan tricks you into losing faith. He makes you believe that the Lord will abandon you. We know this is not true because the Lord says in Joshua 1:5 (NIV), "No one will be able to stand up against you all the days of your life. As I was with Moses, so I will be with you; I will never leave you nor forsake you."

As the first round continues, our fighter maintains his attack with combinations to the head and body. Our fighter's coach is watching and he is pleased with our fighter's performance. Our fighter avoids attacks from his opponent by making him miss punches. As Satan finds it hard to hit us Christians with sin, we tell Satan from Isaiah 54:17 (NIV), "'No weapon forged against you will prevail, and you will refute every tongue that accuses you. This is the heritage of the servants of the LORD, and this is their vindication from me,' declares the LORD." It is very important in the first round of this fight to avoid getting careless. Even though our fighter is hitting our opponent with heavy punches, our fighter must stay focused on the fight plan. As a new believer in the first round of *this twelve-round fight we call life*, it is very important to be mindful of the positions you place yourself into. As new believers, you do not want to give the enemy an opportunity to hurt you. For instance, it is very risky for a boxer to lead punch with a hook because this puts him in a position where he is wide open to be hit. Unless you're Roy Jones, Jr., leave the lead hooks alone.

In your early Christian walk, take one step at a time. A beginner boxer must learn how to make a proper boxing stance, then learns how to step to move around the ring. This alone is practiced for a long period of time before you move on to other maneuvers. A new Christian must learn how to stand in Christ and develop a foundation. You must learn the fundamentals as a Christian before moving on to other areas. A boxer must be fundamentally sound in order to perform at their best abilities. A Christian must be fundamentally sound and grounded in the teachings of the Holy Bible. Being fundamentally sound as a boxer provides an advantage for you when your opponent attempts an attack. You will have the abilities to avoid and defend any attacks and respond with counter punches to protect yourself. Satan will attack you with every weapon in his arsenal. He knows your weaknesses, and he will pursue you from every direction. Satan cannot withstand righteousness. James 4:7 (NIV) boldly states, "Submit yourselves, then, to God. Resist the devil, and he will flee from you." These principles are designed to give you victory in this fight.

First Corinthians 3:10–14 (NIV) says:

> By the grace God has given me, I laid a foundation as an expert builder, and someone else is building on it. But each one should be careful how he builds. For no one can lay any foundation other than the one already laid, which is Jesus Christ. If any man builds on this foundation using gold, silver, costly stones, wood, hay or straw, his work will be shown for what it is, because the Day will

bring it to light. It will be revealed with fire, and the fire will test the quality of each man's work. If what he has built survives, he will receive his reward.

You must build on your proper fundamentals.

Let's get back to the fight. Our opponent throws a right and is warned about hitting the back of the head. They have a nice exchange of punches that come in fast. Our fighter lands a nice jab and follows up with a left hook. Our fighter also sneaks in a jab and then stuns him with a straight right hand. If round one is an indicator of what is to come, this will be a very entertaining fight to watch. Our fighter controls the first half of the round, but our opponent tries to come back but gets out-hustled by our fighter. Our opponent bullies his way inside and causes an intentional head butt against our fighter. There was no damage caused to our fighter. Our opponent was warned about the head butt, and now they're both trying to land on the inside. Our fighter caught our opponent with a left hook and a big right hand to the forehead. Our fighter follows with a blistering left hook that momentarily rocks our opponent who is on the retreat after he was stunned.

A twelve-round boxing match consists of twelve three-minute rounds, which is a total of thirty-six minutes of boxing. For the Christian, *this twelve-round fight we call life* is not twelve three-minute rounds. The rounds for a Christian are broken into *seasons.* As a boxing match progresses in rounds, events in the fight change, and the fighters may need to change their strategies to gain victory. Boxing is very similar to a chess match. It is not just two people punching each other in the head, although that is what happens; it is an evolving contest where detailed plans are designed to best defeat your opponent. These detailed plans can change at a moment's notice, so the fighters must be prepared to adapt to the new game plan. Many times, this intricate planning and fight strategy is taking place when the fighters are fatigued and exhausted. This is why you *must* train and be prepared prior to your fight. Training and preparation for a Christian is reading the Bible and abiding in the word of God through the Holy Scriptures. When Satan sees that you are faithful and obedient in certain areas of your life, he cannot penetrate that covering God has provided for you. Satan then cunningly changes his game plan and attacks other areas of your life. He will attempt to ruin anything he can get his hands on. He has unlimited choices in your life where he can attack. Your health, marriage, finances, job, children, and anything else he can think of destroying, he will. The Bible says in 1 Peter 5:8 (NIV), "Be self-controlled and alert. Your enemy the devil prowls around like a roaring lion looking for someone to devour."

Our fighter gave a great performance in the first round, and he had the crowd excited due to his overwhelming skills along with his hand and foot speed. He managed to impressively out-box our opponent for the course of this round. The new Christian has "spiritually" out-boxed Satan in this first round season of *this twelve-round fight we call life* with their praise, worship, and clean heart in which the Holy Spirit has inspired. The Lord is pleased as you walk the narrow path of righteousness.

As we move close to the end of the first round of this boxing match, our fighter has done well with keeping his opponent away with the correct combinations and confusing angles. The new believer is relentless with the prayer and worship to our Lord and Savior, which is effective in maintaining a strong showing in this first-round season. Satan is currently in the pit of hell throwing temper tantrums over you. Praise the Lord.

KEEP ON KEEPING ON

As the bell rings to begin round two, our fighter's spirits are high due to his performance in the first round. He is feeling at ease and assured. Our opponent lies patient as our fighter exerts his energy, waiting for the right moment to attack. Our opponent steps in close and surprisingly shoots a straight right hand to our fighter's chin, but he missed because our fighter moved his head to the side. In your Christian walk, Satan will shoot the straight right hand of sin and aim for your weakest areas. For the former drug addict, Satan will have you cross paths with your former drug supplier and put you in that "let's get high" situation. Satan will try to seduce you into sin. It says in Matthew 4:8 (NIV), "Again, the devil took him to a very high mountain and showed him all the kingdoms of the world and their splendor." To Satan's dissatisfaction, you stand on faith and the Holy Spirit and decline to engage in your former lifestyle. God is pleased and Satan is in conniption. Revelation 12:17 (NIV) says, "Then the dragon was enraged at the woman and went off to make war against the rest of her offspring—those who obey God's commandments and hold to the testimony of Jesus." Any time you are doing the will of God, Satan is on a warpath to destroy you. The more you worship, the more he attacks. Satan does not have to attack the unsaved because they already belong to him. Satan is out to annihilate your soul.

In this boxing match, both fighters are in peak physical condition and they are both hungry to win. This is one of those fights that are hard to predict because of the high skill levels of each fighter. The winner of this fight will basically boil down to who has the better day or who will let their guard down first. Second Corinthians 10:4–5 (NIV) says:

> The weapons we fight with are not the weapons of the world. On the contrary, they have divine power to demolish strongholds. We demolish arguments and every pretension that sets itself up against the knowledge of God, and we take captive every thought to make it obedient to Christ.

Christians cannot underestimate the abilities of Satan. Second Corinthians 11:14 (NIV) says, "And no wonder, for Satan himself masquerades as an angel of light." Do not be misled by those who speak eloquent words that are not of God. As a young Christian (young not in age, but young in Christ), make it a point to verify any information given to you concerning the Holy Scriptures, which means reading the perfect Word of God (the Holy Bible). It isn't that you shouldn't trust your pastor or people you know when they speak of Scriptures, but reading for yourself gives you empowerment over Satan. Matthew 6:33 (NIV) says, "But seek first his kingdom and his righteousness, and all these things will be given to you as well." Do not blindly believe everything you hear, especially if you do not have the insight of the spoken biblical issue.

As the boxers "mix it up" in the middle of the ring, they are "testing the waters" and assessing the power, speed, and heart of each other as they battle in this contest of will and skill. They are still fresh with the strength and reflexes as they skillfully maneuver around each other scoring back and forth. There is a struggle between the fighters, and they are both looking for the "break" to get them in control of the fight. A new believer will get in struggles with temptations and fleshly things. Hebrews 4:14–16 (NIV) states:

> Therefore, since we have a great high priest who has gone through the heavens, Jesus the Son of God, let us hold firmly to the faith we profess. For we do not have a high priest who is unable to sympathize with our weaknesses, but we have one who has been tempted in every way, just as we

are—yet was without sin. Let us then approach the throne of grace with confidence, so that we may receive mercy and find grace to help us in our time of need.

It's been said that a good leader would not ask anything of his followers that he wouldn't do himself. Jesus Christ epitomizes the military term "lead by example." The Lord isn't expecting anything from us that he didn't require of himself. He knows the struggle, because he has lived it, and favorable for us, he never gave up the struggle. Luke 17:1 (NIV) says, "Jesus said to his disciples: 'Things that cause people to sin are bound to come, but woe to that person through whom they come.'" Jesus Christ knows what it is to be human. He knows how it is to be tempted by any and every evil spirit out there. Luke 4:1–13 (NIV) states:

> Jesus, full of the Holy Spirit, returned from the Jordan and was led by the Spirit in the desert, where for forty days he was tempted by the devil. He ate nothing during those days, and at the end of them he was hungry. The devil said to him, "If you are the Son of God, tell this stone to become bread." Jesus answered, "It is written: 'Man does not live on bread alone.'" The devil led him up to a high place and showed him in an instant all the kingdoms of the world. And he said to him, "I will give you all their authority and splendor, for it has been given to me, and I can give it to anyone I

want to. So if you worship me, it will all be yours." Jesus answered, "It is written: 'Worship the Lord your God and serve him only.'" The devil led him to Jerusalem and had him stand on the highest point of the temple. "If you are the Son of God," he said, "throw yourself down from here. For it is written: 'He will command his angels concerning you to guard you carefully; they will lift you up in their hands, so that you will not strike your foot against a stone.'" Jesus answered, "It says: 'Do not put the Lord your God to the test.'" When the devil had finished all this tempting, he left him until an opportune time.

Christians will encounter struggles in their walks in Christ, but it is not the struggles you experience that are so important, it is how you respond to the struggles. Becoming a disciple of Christ does not give us immunity from life's problems. You may ask, "Why does a loving God allow us to suffer financial hardships, illness, and death if he loves us?" I thought loving us meant he wanted us to live a good, comfortable life. Well, not quite. This is where many people get deceived, and believe God makes sure his believers live the "good life." Doesn't he love us? Yes, he does. John 13:34 (NIV) says, "A new command I give you: Love one another. As I have loved you, so you must love one another." Yup, he loves us.

It says in Romans 8:28 (NIV), "And we know that in all things God works for the good of those who love him, who have been called according to his purpose." The issues we go through in life are part of the working together for his good. So rest assured that all your trials and tribulations are for divine reasons that are beyond our understanding.

Let's get back to the fight. The tempo has picked up and the punches are flowing from both fighters. The crowds are standing and cheering on these two gladiators as they pound each other. Each fighter must be mindful not to get careless and leave an opening that will get them knocked out. Satan is continuously looking for the openings to score the knock out on you. Now, if you get knocked out by Satan in *this twelve-round fight we call life*, this means you have severed your ties with Christ and you die in your sin. When you die in your sin, you belong to Satan. In other words, you fell into the traps that Satan had set for you. Those traps are usually the lifestyles you lived before you came to Christ. Satan can present sin to you in ways that you will not notice. He will attack your weakest areas and exploit your vulnerabilities. If pornography is your weakness, Satan will arrange a pornographic Web page advertisement to pop up on your computer monitor, or the pay-per-view adult movie channel will appear as you surf channels on your television.

Pornography is a poison that is addictive and destructive. It promotes sexual perversion, and sex should only be between a husband and wife.

Pornography gradually grows into other deviant sexual behavior; it's a slippery slope. Romans 6:19 (NIV) says, "I put this in human terms because you are weak in your natural selves. Just as you used to offer the parts of your body in slavery to impurity and to ever-increasing wickedness, so now offer them in slavery to righteousness leading to holiness."

Looking at pornography is adultery. Matthew 5:28 (NIV) says, "But I tell you that anyone who looks at a woman lustfully has already committed adultery with her in his heart." This also applies to women who lust after men.

The sins of pornography can only be subdued from the teachings of the Bible. God clearly says to read the Bible. Second Timothy 3:15–17 (NIV) says:

> … and how from infancy you have known the holy Scriptures, which are able to make you wise for salvation through faith in Christ Jesus. All Scripture is God-breathed and is useful for teaching, rebuking, correcting and training in righteousness, so that the man of God may be thoroughly equipped for every good work.

As you continue in your Christian walk, God's perfect plan for your life will be revealed. The beginning is developing a personal relationship with our Lord and Savior Jesus Christ. Romans 8:1 (NIV) says, "Therefore, there is now no condemnation for those who are in Christ Jesus." Amen to that!

A personal relationship with Christ is not as hard as you may think. There is no magic "heebie jeebie" or mysterious activities that need to take place. Once we become a child of the living God, the Holy Spirit will begin to work on our hearts. We should pray, pray and pray, and join a Bible believing church. You will begin to grow spiritually. Your faith and trust in God will get you through any life situation, and believing that he is your sustainer is the way to have a relationship with him. Although you may not see changes immediately, you will begin to see them over time, and all the truths will become clearer.

As the boxing match continues, the left jab has become very effective for our fighter. The jab is keeping our opponent off balance and scoring points. A jab is designed to keep the opponent on the defense and distracts from their game plan. Many boxing matches have been won utilizing the jab. The jab is also used to set up an attack on your opponent. Many times, a boxer will jab their way inside to get close to the opponent, so they can unleash the power punches. As a Christian, Satan is always trying to jab his way in to attack your life. One way he attacks is through peer-pressure. A peer seems to be harmless because they are your friends, co-workers, relatives, and any other person you interact with. With peers, you may have your guard down because they are someone you may have a degree of trust with. The Bible tells us that we should not expect our lives to look like the lives of other people in this world (unbelievers). Second Peter 2:11(NIV) says, "Bold and arrogant, these men are not afraid to slander celestial beings; yet even angels, although they are stronger and more powerful, do not bring slanderous accusations against such beings in the presence of the Lord." As Christians, we are misfits and foreigners here on earth. Just as Christ was disdained (and still is) by so many people who wanted to live their lives their own way, so are we for being followers. Romans 12:2 (NIV) instructs, "Do not conform any longer to the pattern of this world, but be transformed by the renewing of your mind. Then you will be able to test and approve what God's will is—his good, pleasing and perfect will."

Peer pressure will last for a limited time, a transient element in your lives. Giving in to peer pressure is mostly about insecurity and the passion for acceptance from people who don't care about you. First Corinthians 10:13 (NIV) re-assures us with, "No temptation has seized you except what is common to man. And God is faithful; he will not let you be tempted beyond what you can bear. But when you are tempted, he will also provide a way out so that you can stand up under it."

God will not let us bear any more than we can handle, and *he* always gives us a way out of committing sin. Do not give in to your weaknesses and submit to peer-pressure. Sometimes, a change in the friends you keep is what should take place. When you keep company with other believers, that peer pressure turns in to a "pure pressure." The influence of drug use, fornication, and telling lies on others turns into getting high off of the Holy Spirit, meaningful relationships, and encouraging others. Standing up for what we believe in the Bible pleases God. Never apologize for being a Christian.

Our fighter has done well this round with the stiff jabs to keep his opponent away. There were some moments when our fighter looked to be in trouble, but as God promised, he found a way out. In the second-round season of *this twelve-round fight we call life,* our new believer escaped the traps of Satan by resisting the temptations of sin from personal weaknesses and peer-pressure. Every triumph in the Lord increases righteousness. Matthew 5:6 (NIV) says, "Blessed are those who hunger and thirst for righteousness, for they will be filled."

SIN IS SIN

The bell rings to begin the third round. Our fighter is pushing our opponent around the ring, landing combinations anytime the opponent tries to come forward, and pressuring our opponent backwards. Our fighter was so confident and in control of the fight that he began to showboat. When a Christian has consecutive spiritual warfare victories over Satan, an over-confident attitude may set inside the heart of the Christian. As the Good Lord sees fit, a believer can win battles against Satan over and over again, which proves that the Lord of Lords, King of Kings is real. There are many Christians who receive divine favor, and continue to acknowledge the source of their blessings (Jesus Christ). There are also Christians who receive divine favor and gradually forget where their blessings came from. Some believers may start to give themselves the credit for the achievements in their lives and forget about the God who supplied the blessings to them. When this happens, this confidence can turn into arrogance or conceit. The Bible talks about the *parable of the Pharisee and the tax collector*. Luke 18:9–14 (NIV) says:

> To some who were confident of their own righteousness and looked down on everybody else, Jesus told this parable: "Two men went up to the temple to pray, one a Pharisee and the other a tax collector. The Pharisee stood up and prayed about himself: 'God, I thank you that I am not like other men—robbers, evildoers, adulterers—or even like this tax collector. I fast twice a week and give a tenth of all I get.'

> "But the tax collector stood at a distance. He would not even look up to heaven, but beat his breast and said, 'God, have mercy on me, a sinner.'

> "I tell you that this man, rather than the other, went home justified before God. For everyone who exalts himself will be humbled, and he who humbles himself will be exalted."

Vast wealth and extraordinary abilities will not protect those who turn from God. What he made, he can take. The good news of it all, however, is that it is never too late to turn to God. He will always forgive and protect those who truly repent. *Websters Dictionary* defines "repent" as "to turn from sin and dedicate oneself to the amendment of one's life."

Acts 3:19 (NIV) says, "Repent, then, and turn to God, so that your sins may be wiped out, that times of refreshing may come from the Lord." A change of mind will result in a change of behavior.

Our fighter is spending unnecessary energy on being "flashy" against an opponent who is focused on winning. Although our fighter is winning at this point, he is taking needless risks that can get him hurt. Our opponent works his way inside and lands hard body shots, causing our fighter to back up against the ropes for the first time of the fight. While on the ropes, our fighter tries to block the hard punches that are digging into his mid-section, but he cannot deter this body attack. Our fighter is about to get in a dangerous situation as he continues to remain against the ropes. In a desperate measure, our fighter reaches out, and wraps his arms around our opponent and holds on for dear life. Our opponent continues punching while being held, and the referee, all of a sudden, steps in to break the fighters up. Our fighter is relieved for a moment as the referee separates the two boxers. This brief split gave our fighter a moment to get his thoughts together and recover from the body attack.

For a Christian, our spiritual referee is Jesus Christ via intercessory prayer. He, all of a sudden, steps in and gives us relief when the times get too rough. Intercessory prayer is the act of praying on behalf of others. Jesus Christ became the avenue to

God for us when *he* died on the cross. *He* was the greatest mediator that ever lived. Now, we can intercede in prayer for other Christians or the unsaved and pray for their salvation in God's due time. First Timothy 2:5 (NIV) says, "For there is one God and one mediator between God and men, the man Christ Jesus." The Bible implicitly states that all Christians are summoned to be intercessors. Christians possess the Holy Spirit, and as *he* intercedes for us, we are commanded to intercede for others. First Samuel 12:23 (NIV) says, "As for me, far be it from me that I should sin against the LORD by failing to pray for you. And I will teach you the way that is good and right." It is our duty to pray for others.

The brief, sudden interruption made by the referee as he broke the fighters up bought our fighter enough time to recover from the body attack. Our fighter has collected his thoughts and is back to fighting the way he trained. Our fighter changed his ways and has re-gained control of the fight. Our fighter was feeling overwhelmed due to the heavy attack he received.

There may be times when you feel overwhelmed in your life. There are moments when you may feel like life is beating you up. You may feel that everything is coming down on you and you cannot do anything about it. James 1:12 (NIV) assures us, "Blessed is the man who perseveres under trial, because when he has stood the test, he will receive the crown of life that God has promised to those who love him." God gives us the strength to withstand any adversary, whether it's temptation or tragedy. We need to believe in his power and authority in order to receive the full effect of his grace.

Mark 11:22–24 (NIV) says:

"Have faith in God," Jesus answered. "I tell you the truth, if anyone says to this mountain, 'Go, throw yourself into the sea,' and does not doubt in his heart but believes that what he says will happen, it will be done for him. Therefore I tell you, whatever you ask for in prayer, believe that you have received it, and it will be yours."

Jesus also said in Matthew 17:20 (NIV), "He replied, 'Because you have so little faith. I tell you the truth, if you have faith as small as a mustard seed, you can say to this mountain, "Move from here to there" and it will move. Nothing will be impossible for you.'"

That is some heavy duty power through Christ. We can move mountains if we believe in him. Don't worry about how the mountain is going to move, just believe it will move.

Our fighter has stopped clowning around and begun to take the fight seriously, since his pummeling. Uppercuts and hooks are connecting with great force to the opponent's head. Our opponent has blood pouring from his mouth at this time. Both fighters are trading furious blows, and the crowds are screaming and cheering to this intense action. This is what a fighter anticipates when they train for a fight. All the hard training is to prepare to get into a "dog fight." It is obvious these two boxers are in phenomenal condition, judging from the pace they have set. Through this action, they have set a precedent of what is to come in this fight.

As Christians, the Lord has set a precedent on what we are to expect as believers. Malachi 3:1 (NIV) says, "See, I will send my messenger, who will prepare the way before me. Then suddenly the Lord you are seeking will come to his temple; the messenger of the covenant, whom you desire, will come," says the LORD Almighty."

We can expect a fulfilling life, as long as you believe. Wealth and status does not define a fulfilling life. There are many wealthy people who commit suicide and suffer from depression. You hear on a daily basis in the news about wealthy celebrities who get divorced or get admitted to drug rehab. As the old saying goes, "Money does not buy happiness." Matthew 19:24 (NIV) plainly says, "Again I tell you, it is easier for a camel to go through the eye of a needle than for a rich man to enter the kingdom of God."

This verse was not speaking primarily on wealth, but Christ was focused on an attitude that directed faith and obedience to our heavenly Father. Matthew 16:26–27 (NIV) also says, "What good will it be for a man if he gains the whole world, yet forfeits his soul? Or what can a man give in exchange for his soul? For the Son of Man is going to come in his Father's glory with his angels, and then he will reward each person according to what he has done."

God does not need your money! He wants your soul. He desires to be your number one resource. He aspires to comfort you during rough times. He loves you. Job 16:15, "But my mouth would encourage you; comfort from my lips would bring you relief."

Since the moment man "fell" and became disobedient to God, we have been undeserving of his grace and mercy. Jeremiah 17:9 (NIV) says, "The heart is deceitful above all things and beyond cure. Who can understand it?" How can God love a wicked heart? It says in 1 John 4:8 (NIV), "Whoever does not love does not know God, because God is love." This scripture is very deep because God doesn't just love, he is love. Love isn't what he can do, it is what he is. His entire substance is love. My small brain finds it hard to comprehend, but it says in 1 Corinthians 13:4–13 (NIV):

> Love is patient, love is kind. It does not envy, it does not boast, it is not proud. It is not rude, it is not self-seeking, it is not easily angered, it keeps no record of wrongs. Love does not delight in evil but rejoices with the truth. It always protects, always trusts, always hopes, always perseveres.
>
> Love never fails. But where there are prophecies,

they will cease; where there are tongues, they will be stilled; where there is knowledge, it will pass away. For we know in part and we prophesy in part, but when perfection comes, the imperfect disappears. When I was a child, I talked like a child, I thought like a child, I reasoned like a child. When I became a man, I put childish ways behind me. Now we see but a poor reflection as in a mirror; then we shall see face to face. Now I know in part; then I shall know fully, even as I am fully known. And now these three remain: faith, hope and love. But the greatest of these is love.

Since God's true nature is love, it is his character to love all. For even the most undeserving people, he has chosen to bestow is unchanging love, even though we rebel against him. First John 4:10 (NIV) says about God's love, "This is love: not that we loved God, but that he loved us and sent his Son as an atoning sacrifice for our sins." He loved us when we did not love him. He loved us when we disobeyed his commandments. He loved us when we placed other items in our lives before him. He loves us yesterday, today, and forevermore.

Getting back to the fight, these two fighters are in the heat of battle, displaying courage and physical strength. Our opponent caught our fighter with a strong right hand and a left hook to the chin, putting our fighter down on the canvas. The referee counts, "One, two, three." Our fighter pops up quickly, but his legs are unsteady. Our fighter holds on for dear life, and the opponent sends a grazing right to the top of our fighter's head, causing him to stumble halfway across the ring, but then he miraculously regains his composure. By the end of the round, our fighter appears steady, but he is on shaky ground.

We, as Christians, can get disoriented in our walk, just like our fighter who became unstable, but he regained his composure in the nick of time.

Second Peter 3:16 (NIV) says, "He writes the same way in all his letters, speaking in them of these matters. His letters contain some things that are hard to understand, which ignorant and unstable people distort, as they do the other Scriptures, to their own destruction." Many "so-called" believers distort the Holy Scriptures to suit their personal agenda. They obey some scriptures, but ignore others. This causes many believers to live sinful lifestyles, which caused them to ride on a fast track to the lake of fire, and they don't even know it.

For instance, a homosexual lifestyle is not what God intended for his children. First Corinthians 6:9–10 (NIV) says:

> Do you not know that the wicked will not inherit the kingdom of God? Do not be deceived: Neither the sexually immoral nor idolaters nor adulterers nor male prostitutes nor homosexual offenders nor thieves nor the greedy nor drunkards nor slanderers nor swindlers will inherit the kingdom of God.

In the 1970s, homosexuality was considered a psychological disorder. Nowadays, it is considered normal and acceptable. Many people "believe" they are born a homosexual. Romans 1:26–27 (NIV) says:

> Because of this, God gave them over to shameful lusts. Even their women exchanged natural relations for unnatural ones. In the same way the men also abandoned natural relations with women and were inflamed with lust for one another. Men committed indecent acts with other men, and received in themselves the due penalty for their perversion.

If you believe in God and the Bible, then you cannot ignore the plain language the Bible refers to homosexual behavior. These behaviors are a "struggle," a sin, just like any other issue in life. Alcoholism, drug abuse, and uncontrollable anger are all forms of sin that we need deliverance from. Homosexuality is in the same category, a sin. In 1 John 1:8–10 (NIV) it says:

> If we claim to be without sin, we deceive ourselves and the truth is not in us. If we confess our sins, he is faithful and just and will forgive us our sins and purify us from all unrighteousness. If we claim we have not sinned, we make him out to be a liar and his word has no place in our lives.

The Bible states that no Christian is sinless and all Christians occasionally fail in those struggles. Ephesians 1:13-14 (NIV) says, "And you also were included in Christ when you heard the word of truth, the gospel of your salvation. Having believed, you were marked in him with a seal, the promised Holy Spirit, who is a deposit guaranteeing our inheritance until the redemption of those who are God's possession—to the praise of his glory." Just like our fighter who was knocked down, he got up. When we fall to sin, we must spiritually "get up" and repent so that we may be forgiven.

Our fighter took a pretty good beating this round, but he made it through. In our Christian walk, we sometimes take beatings. If God brought you to it, he will bring you through it. Psalm 23:4 (NIV) reassures us with, "Even though I walk through the valley of the shadow of death, I will fear no evil, for you are with me; your rod and your staff, they comfort me." It also says in Joshua 1:9 (NIV), "Have I not commanded you? Be strong and courageous. Do not be terrified; do not be discouraged, for the LORD your God will be with you wherever you go." Always know that he is with you at all times.

As a Christian, you are never alone. Psalm 91:11 (NIV) says, "For he will command his angels concerning you to guard you in all your ways." In other words, you are always protected. God has your back with his angels assigned to only you, for your protection. The Secret Service has nothing on the protection of God's angels.

The third-round season of *this twelve-round fight we call life* has seen some challenges, but the almighty God is faithful to preserve us as he desires. Blessed is the name of the Lord.

"BLINDED BY SATAN"

As the bell rings to start round four, our fighter immediately took control by circling, jabbing, and throwing combinations while our opponent seemed content to throw one-twos. An intentional head butt opened a cut over the right eye of our fighter that grew into a bloody gash. The referee penalized the opponent and deducted a point on the scorecards.

Just like our opponent in the boxing match played dirty with the head butt, Satan can and does play "dirty" for the purpose of causing you harm. The Bible says in Genesis 3:1–6 (NIV):

> Now the serpent was more crafty than any of the wild animals the LORD God had made. He said to the woman, "Did God really say, 'You must not eat from any tree in the garden'?"

The woman said to the serpent, "We may eat fruit from the trees in the garden, but God did say, 'You must not eat fruit from the tree that is in the middle of the garden, and you must not touch it, or you will die.'"

"You will not surely die," the serpent said to the woman. "For God knows that when you eat of it your eyes will be opened, and you will be like God, knowing good and evil."

When the woman saw that the fruit of the tree was good for food and pleasing to the eye, and also desirable for gaining wisdom, she took some and ate it. She also gave some to her husband, who was with her, and he ate it.

Satan played "dirty" and succeeded in tricking Eve. Satan is the king of lies. He takes pleasure in the suffering of others. The good news is that we have a Savior who is stronger than Satan. One who will come to destroy the enemy and redeem his people to their rightful place.

Romans 8:31–32 (NIV) says, "What, then, shall we say in response to this? If God is for us, who can be against us? He who did not spare his own Son, but gave him up for us all—how will he not also, along with him, graciously give us all things?" It doesn't matter what challenges or problems you face because our Lord Jesus Christ is in control of everything. Whoever has an animosity toward you, whether it's a family member or a friend, God is in control. If God is for you, do not consider who is against you. The greatness of his mercy overwhelms the enemy.

Let's get back to the fight. Our fighter responded to the intentional head-butt with a hard right hand over the top, connecting on the left temple. Our fighter pumped his jab several times, and he showed superior hand speed, especially with his lead left, although blood poured from his eye. Our opponent landed two or three decent right hands, but our fighter kept controlling the tempo. Blood is pouring from our fighter's right eye, and it is affecting his vision. Our fighter is finding it hard to see the punches that are hitting him.

There are times when Satan blinds our eyes with "circumstances," in an attempt to prevent us from seeing God. For instance, an unplanned pregnancy is a very delicate and sensitive issue for anyone. If you are about to graduate college or you just started that new and exciting job, you may be thinking to yourself, *This is a bad time to get pregnant.* You may contemplate abortion. Satan has convinced many people to believe that an abortion is "women's health care." I always thought health care involved saving lives, not taking lives. Exodus 20:13 (NIV) says, "You shall not murder." *Websters Dictionary* defines murder as, "the crime of unlawfully killing a person especially with malice aforethought." Exodus 21:22–25 (NIV) speaks directly about abortion:

If men who are fighting hit a pregnant woman and she gives birth prematurely but there is no serious injury, the offender must be fined whatever the woman's husband demands and the court allows. But if there is serious injury, you are to take life for life, eye for eye, tooth for tooth, hand for hand, foot for foot, burn for burn, wound for wound, bruise for bruise.

The Bible calls for the same punishment for murdering an unborn baby, as murdering an adult. Genesis 1:26–27 (NIV) delightfully says:

Then God said, "Let us make man in our image, in our likeness, and let them rule over the fish of the sea and the birds of the air, over the livestock, over all the earth, and over all the creatures that move along the ground." So God created man in his own image, in the image of God he created him; male and female he created them.

I am made in his image? That alone is enough to jump for joy!

Jeremiah 1:5 (NIV) illustrates that God knew us before we were conceived: "Before I formed you in the womb I knew you, before you were born I set you apart; I appointed you as a prophet to the nations." The "so-called" brilliant legal minds of the United States Supreme Court got this one totally wrong concerning abortion. All because abortion is legal, that does not make it right. In Psalm 94:20–21 (NIV) tells about the evils of some laws, "Can a corrupt throne be allied with you—one that brings on misery by its decrees? They band together against the righteous and condemn the innocent to death." There are many laws that protect innocent victims of crimes. People go to jail all the time for assaults and other crimes against persons. How can the destruction of an unborn child be deemed legal?

There are alternatives to abortion. A woman who kills her unborn child will have to live with the consequences for the rest of her life. Many women experience guilt, post-abortion stress syndrome, and depression. Just imagine all of the prophets, angels, pastors, presidents, generals, and doctors who were murdered out of convenience. If you think about it, abortion is one of the reasons why there are so few young people paying into Social Security. It's because they were never given a chance to exist and become tax payers. Abortion is a sin, and this sin can be forgiven through faith in Christ. If any man paid for, or encouraged an abortion, that is a sin. Doctors who perform abortions are committing sin. Abortion is not any less forgivable than any other sin, but you must repent.

For any woman who has had an abortion, the world has not ended for you. Romans 8:1 (NIV) says, "Therefore, there is now no condemnation for those who are in Christ Jesus."

For women who have experienced abortion, do

not allow Satan to bring you down. Use this event to help others make a better decision. An abortion can be very traumatic, but trusting in the Lord during these times will make you spiritually stronger. It is occurrences like this, where God enables us to minister to others and use these bad events to serve as a blessing to other women in similar situations.

I see abortion as one "tool" used by the modern feminist movement which sends the message that "a man cannot tell a woman what to do with her body." I see the modern feminist movement as a notion straight from the depths of hell. This movement started as a positive element of our society, fighting for women's rights that God intended for us all to have. We know the Bible intends for women to live equally. God sees man and woman as equal members in the Body of Christ. Galatians 3:28 (NIV) says, "There is neither Jew nor Greek, slave nor free, male nor female, for you are all one in Christ Jesus."

God does not discriminate on who he wants to worship him. He requires all to worship him. In my view, feminism has gone beyond the true intentions in which God has for women. It appears the modern feminist movement has an apparent arrogant spirit attached to it. It promotes a self-serving and rebellious tone that can drown out the word of God. Some derivatives of the modern feminist movement are destroyed marriages and the lack of respect for human life. Pride is what the modern feminist movement fuels from, and we know that the proud shall fall. Proverbs 16:18 (NIV) says, "Pride goes before destruction, a haughty spirit before a fall." Inequality to any segment to our society is a sin. You cannot defeat sin with sin; it requires the mighty hand of God to change hearts.

Back to the fight. Our fighter's left hand becomes most effective in this round, as he landed jabs and hooks. Our opponent's determination and conditioning shows up here, and he continues to walk our fighter down. Our fighter is beginning to look a little winded. As the fighters battle in close, our opponent says to our fighter, "You're tired and your eye is badly cut; you should give up because you have no chance of winning. You're of no more value in this fight. There is nothing else you can do, just give up." Our opponent is basically saying that it is not worth it for our fighter to continue the fight.

The scenario in this stage of the fight calls to mind the issue of euthanasia. Our fighter is being told that he is unable to win because of his fatigue and cut eye. Our fighter is being encouraged to "give up." Euthanasia is defined in *Webster's Dictionary* as "the act or method of causing death painlessly, so as to end suffering; advocated by some as a way to deal with persons dying of incurable, painful diseases."

There are serious repercussions when "man plays God" in issues of life and death. As the old saying goes, "The past is history, the future is a mystery, but today is a gift, that's why we call it the present." So many Christians would say that our lives are the most valued gift that God has given us, with the privilege to worship and be a part of God's everlasting plan for his children. After all, we are all made in his image.

Concerning euthanasia, Deuteronomy 30:19–20 (NIV) says:

> This day I call heaven and earth as witnesses against you that I have set before you life and death, blessings and curses. Now choose life, so that you and your children may live and that you may love the LORD your God, listen to his voice, and hold fast to him. For the LORD is your life, and he will give you many years in the land he swore to give to your fathers, Abraham, Isaac and Jacob.

> And that you may love the LORD your God, listen to his voice, and hold fast to him. For the LORD is your life, and he will give you many years in the land he swore to give to your fathers, Abraham, Isaac and Jacob.

God already has your days numbered. Euthanasia prevents God from doing his work. God's time to heal an incapacitated person may not have come to pass. Therefore, God is cut out of this healing equation. When a person causes the death of another via euthanasia, it is murder. Here it is again in Exodus 20:13 (NIV), "You shall not murder."

The bell rang to end round four, and both fighters went back to their corners with battle scars. For the Christian, the fourth-round season of *this twelve-round fight we call life* has dealt some serious blows. Abortion can and will cause more than physiological damage to a woman's body. It can adversely affect many psychological and emotional areas of a woman's life. Euthanasia is the act of taking matters into your own hands when God already has a plan that is better than yours. Our great country must account for the millions of deaths committed through abortion and euthanasia that have been authorized by our government. We reap what we sow in our deeds. This indeed, displays that a climate of death has plagued our wonderful country.

TEMPTATIONS LURK

At the beginning of the round, our opponent came out stalking and pressuring our fighter, but he could not trap him in the corner as intended. Our opponent's jab picked up steam, and he was able to work his way inside for the body attack on our fighter. About halfway through the round, our opponent landed a monstrous straight right hand to our fighter's chin that backed him into the blue corner, the opponent's corner. Our opponent moved in and landed a crunching left uppercut, and when our fighter didn't go down, our opponent obliged him with a right uppercut. Our fighter was effectively out on his feet but threw punches until the referee stepped in and gave a standing eight count. After the referee finished the eight count, the referee pulled our fighter close and whispered in his ear. The referee said to our fighter, "The promoter will double your purse if you give the fight up. This is the most money you will ever see if you just go down. You're getting badly beaten and it's only going to get worse. Just lay down and the punishment will be over." This is a major temptation for our fighter, being he has been severely battered and this would be the most money he had ever seen. All he has to do is give up the fight.

We Christians are confronted with temptations to "give up" from Satan every day. As described in the fight above, our fighter is tempted to take a "dive," and purposely lose the fight. In *this twelve-round fight we call life*, when we take a "dive," that means we lose the fight. When we lose the fight, that means we die in our sins. The above fight scenario would describe the equivalent to committing suicide for the Christian. Suicide does not solve anything; it only causes more tragedy and suffering. There is no issue in your life that God cannot bring you through. Ecclesiastes 7:17 (NIV) says, "Do not be overwicked, and do not be a fool—why die before your time?" If you consider suicide as an option or know someone who committed suicide, Jesus Christ wants you to know that there is always hope, and he is the wonderful healer that can renew your life. There were many great persons of the Bible who suffered severe depression and thoughts of suicide.

It is written about King David in Psalms 13:2–4 (NIV):

How long must I wrestle with my thoughts and every day have sorrow in my heart? How long will my enemy triumph over me? Look on me and answer, O LORD my God. Give light to my eyes, or I will sleep in death; my enemy will say, "I have overcome him," and my foes will rejoice when I fall.

King David was ready to "throw in the towel."

The prophet Jeremiah expressed his grief in Jeremiah 20:14–18(NIV):

Cursed be the day I was born! May the day my mother bore me not be blessed! Cursed be the man who brought my father the news, who made him very glad, saying, "A child is born to you—a son!" May that man be like the towns the LORD overthrew without pity. May he hear wailing in the morning, a battle cry at noon. For he did not kill me in the womb, with my mother as my grave, her womb enlarged forever. Why did I ever come out of the womb to see trouble and sorrow and to end my days in shame?

One more example of our admirable men of the Bible who suffered times of great hardship and depression in their lives. Job 7:15–16 (NIV) says, "So that I prefer strangling and death, rather than this body of mine. I despise my life; I would not live forever. Let me alone; my days have no meaning." These men were tremendously blessed by God, and they persevered through their suffering and injustice, because they believed in the Lord with all their hearts.

Suicide is not an indefensible sin, but the concern is at the time of a suicide, had that individual dissolved their relationship with Christ? Mark 3:28 (NIV) says, "I tell you the truth, all the sins and blasphemies of men will be forgiven them." Sins are forgiven if you have a relationship with Christ.

The only unforgivable sin is blasphemy of the Holy Spirit: Mark 3:29 (NIV) says about blasphemy, "But whoever blasphemes against the Holy Spirit will never be forgiven; he is guilty of an eternal sin."

Mark 16:16 (NIV) says, "Whoever believes and is baptized will be saved, but whoever does not believe will be condemned." If you do not believe, you are rejecting Christ.

You can turn your life around by submitting to God and allow him to govern your life. Suicide should never be an option. God can set you free from any and all evil thoughts of suicide. It says in Romans 12:2 (NIV), "Do not conform any longer to the pattern of this world, but be transformed by the renewing of your mind. Then you will be able to test and approve what God's will is—his good, pleasing and perfect will." God has awesome plans for your life; all you have to do is seek his will for you.

Satan is persistent in tempting you. God has dispatched his angels to protect us in every area of our lives. God will not allow Satan to tempt you with more than you can handle. Job 1:10 (NIV) says, "Have you not put a hedge around him and his household and everything he has? You have blessed the work of his hands, so that his flocks and herds are spread throughout the land."

Satan cannot get to you unless God lets him. From this passage, it was clear that Satan tried to attack Job and was not able to, due to God's protection. God removed the protection he had around Job and allowed Satan to attack. God knew Job was spiritually strong enough to withstand the temptations brought by Satan, and he resisted Satan.

Always know that God is with you in every step of your trials. James 1:2–4 (NIV) says, "Consider it pure joy, my brothers, whenever you face trials of many kinds, because you know that the testing of your faith develops perseverance. Perseverance must finish its work so that you may be mature and complete, not lacking anything."

Your trials must take the full course in order for you to develop in Christ. When your trials go beyond your expected time period, that is the time to "bite down" and persevere. Always know that God is with you, and you will be better off in the end.

Let's get back to the fight. Our fighter did not acquiesce to the referee's despicable offer to "throw" the fight. Our fighter instead, decided to "push" through this onslaught of infliction from the opponent. The referee motioned for both fighters to resume the fight. The two fighters brought the full capacity crowd to its feet with blistering back-and-forth action at the center of the ring. Our opponent began to show fatigue, and our fighter saw this and exploded with a burst of punches to the head of our opponent, causing the opponent to stagger back against the ropes covering his face with his gloves. Our fighter delivered a straight right hand to the bridge of our opponent's nose, causing a fracture and severe bleeding. As our fighter continued to viciously punch our opponent, the bell rang to end the round. Both fighters had to be escorted back to their corners because they were disoriented to where they were.

The apostle Paul said in 1 Corinthians 2:2 (NIV), "For I resolved to know nothing while I was with you except Jesus Christ and him crucified." This verse describes that Paul was totally focused on Jesus no matter what afflictions he was going through, as our fighter was totally focused on pressing forward in this fight and blocked out any elements that may distract from winning. The exhaustion and pain did not prevent our fighter from remaining centered on his will to win.

Both boxers in this fight are giving all they got, and they are determined to win. We have seen the tides turn for each boxer, and the courage of each boxer has been tested. It usually comes down to which fighter has the stronger desire to win.

As we continue in *this twelve-round fight we call life*, our level of determination plays a factor as to whether we continue to fight or if we give up and lay down. Our fighter did the right thing and persisted through.

THE FIGHT DOESN'T START TILL YOU GET TIRED

In the course of a boxing match, a fighter shows their true character in times when the going gets tough. In the early rounds of a fight, boxers are able to maneuver and respond however they want because they are still fresh and full of energy. Their reflexes are sharp, and their muscles are strong. Fighters can physically do what they want to do early in a fight. The real "fight" doesn't start until that fatigue begins to set it.

During the middle rounds of a fight, a fighter may get bored and/or fatigued at this point. These are the rounds that indicate the true conditioning of a fighter. The two fighters meet in the middle of the ring to "slug it out" when the bell rings to begin round six. The first minute of the round was pretty close. Our fighter landed a few stiff jabs and caught our opponent with a left hook to his chin that caused his mouthpiece to fly into the third row of the audience. Blood and sweat are literally flying around the ring as both fighters slug each other with fierceness. Our opponent unloads a vicious right uppercut that hurts our fighter as he leans in. Our fighter's legs buckle, and he holds on to our opponent. Our opponent goes for a savage right hand but misses … then comes back a few seconds later and lands two hard body shots. He jabs through our fighter's guard but couldn't get in other shots to finish off our fighter. Our fighter is breathing hard, and his legs look weak as he is taking ferocious shots to the head and body.

Believers go through rounds in *this twelve-round fight we call life* where weariness and worry begin to surface. If you haven't been there, just keep on living. Matthew 11:28–30 (NIV) says, "Come to me, all you who are weary and burdened, and I will give you rest. Take my yoke upon you and learn from me, for I am gentle and humble in heart, and you will find rest for your souls. For my yoke is easy and my burden is light." There are times when "life" can make you feel helpless and overwhelmed. The issues of our lives continue to pile up, and there seems to be no remedy in sight. Finances, health problems, and job issues are earthly reasons for worry. Our burdens increase, thus causing additional anguish to our lives. First Peter 5:6 (NIV) says, "Humble yourselves, therefore, under

God's mighty hand, that he may lift you up in due time. Cast all your anxiety on him because he cares for you." The release is not on your time; it's on his time. You continue to be faithful, and he will provide.

When God says he cares for you, that's much more than when your friend says they care for you. God gave you life; he created you. He cares for you on a level that we cannot comprehend. Have you ever created a project or cooked an extravagant meal with all the fixings from scratch? You know something you did that required an effort from your heart. I'm sure there was a feeling of pride and accomplishment in that task once you completed it. That is how God looks at us. We are his prized possession, the apple of his eye. It says in Ephesians 2:10 (NIV), "For we are God's workmanship, created in Christ Jesus to do good works, which God prepared in advance for us to do." If we believe in God and his Word, there is no reason for any believer to worry about anything.

Matthew 6:25–27 (NIV) says:

> Therefore I tell you, do not worry about your life, what you will eat or drink; or about your body, what you will wear. Is not life more important than food, and the body more important than clothes? Look at the birds of the air; they do not sow or reap or store away in barns, and yet your heavenly Father feeds them. Are you not much more valuable than they? Who of you by worrying can add a single hour to his life?

God provides for the birds of the air, and he will surely provide for you and I.

As the boxing match continues, our fighter begins to show less activity in the heat of battle. It appears our fighter has become bored and lazy in these middle rounds.

When we see life in a static format, it can become boring. Boredom is the result of inactivity. Inactivity can breed a lazy spirit. Proverbs 13:4 (NIV) says, "The sluggard craves and gets nothing, but the desires of the diligent are fully satisfied." If our fighter wants to win, he's going to have to start working.

In the final part of the round, our fighter realizes that he needs to make something happen, and he clearly gets in the better action here … landing a hard left hand body shot and a hard left hook in between our opponents punching. He also lands a short straight left hand and some crisp jabs as well. Our opponent lands a couple of insignificant punches … a small right hand over the top that didn't do anything. Our fighter seems to know that he needs to put forth an extra effort in this fight.

Sometimes Christians feel they are not getting their return on the praise they give God. We do not worship a God who owes us anything. His blessings come in his time, not ours. If God stopped blessing us, we cannot thank him enough for what he has already done. Jeremiah 31:2 (NIV) says, "This is what the LORD says: 'The people who survive the sword will find favor in the desert; I will come to give rest to Israel.'" Don't worry about how much work you do in the name of the Lord, just do the work. God will give you rest.

It's easy to give praise when your life is going well for you. The real test of faith is when your life is turned upside down, and you continue to give praise. Second Corinthians 13:5 (NIV) addresses this: "Examine yourselves to see whether you are in the faith; test yourselves. Do you not realize that Christ Jesus is in you—unless, of course, you fail the test?"

Keep on fighting, no matter what the circumstances are. The breakthrough will eventually come in God's due time.

As we close round six of *this twelve-round fight we call life*, we had focused on the endurance of our faith in the midst of trials. Our faith can weaken during prolonged periods of hardship and grief. First Peter 5:9 (NIV) says, "Resist him, standing firm in the faith, because you know that your brothers throughout the world are undergoing the same kind of sufferings." You are not alone.

This chapter is to encourage our readers to remain fixed on God. We must run this race with endurance as it says in Hebrews 12:1 (NIV): "Therefore, since we are surrounded by such a great cloud of witnesses, let us throw off everything that hinders and the sin that so easily entangles, and let us run with perseverance the race marked out for us."

ONE-MINUTE REST PERIOD

After each round, there is a one-minute rest period. This period of time is meant for the fighter to sit down on a stool and get some rest. This is also a time when the fighter will hydrate by drinking water and cool off with an ice pack placed on the back of his neck or the top of his head. The fighter will also receive instructions from his coach. The coach will give the fighter a strategy that he should take into the next round, in order to win the fight. The coach will also tell the fighter what he is doing wrong so to prevent the fighter from repeating the same mistakes. By the end of the one-minute rest, a fighter should be refreshed and recovered to go back into the fight with a fresh energy. Sometimes a fighter does not want to sit down or listen to the instructions of the coach. This type of fighter wants to do it his way in the ring and refuses to receive instructions from the coach. Rebelling against the coach can cause serious consequences for a fighter because the coach can see things inside the ring that you as the fighter cannot.

For us Christians, we also have a version of the one-minute rest period. There are times when we need to meditate in prayer, our private one-on-one time with God. Those occasions when we attend worship services at your church home. The Sunday school class we attend or teach. The Wednesday night Bible study group. The fellowship with other believers. The times we sing to the Lord and read scriptures. These are some methods that prepare us to get back into the fight of *this twelve-round fight we call life*, with a fresh spirit. There are times when a Christian does not listen to what God is telling them, and they want to do things their way. Christians can be rebellious against what God is telling them, and that can be extremely detrimental. Just as the boxing coach can see things inside the ring that the fighter cannot, God sees areas of your life that you cannot see. You cannot hide anything from God; he sees and knows all. Jeremiah 10:12 (NIV) says about the knowledge of God, "But God made the earth by his power; he founded the world by his wisdom and stretched out the heavens by his understanding." He knows the number of hairs on the top of your head. He knows your every thought. He knows more about you than you know about yourself.

STAY ON THE WALL

Our fighter begins the round in the center of the ring prepared to "duke it out." Both fighters trade shots, but our fighter has more "sting" in his punches, causing the crowd to begin chanting our fighter's name. The cut over our fighter's eye has not been a factor because of the "cut man" and his expertise. Our fighter pumps his jab upstairs and downstairs. He fakes the jab and causes the opponent to move his hand. Our fighter then lands an overhand right to the chin of our opponent, followed by a left hook. Our opponent falls to the canvas with a loud thud as our fighter stands over him. The referee pushes our fighter back and begins the count to ten. On the count of six, our opponent stands to his feet and wobbles backward to the ropes. At the count of nine, he appears stable. The referee lets the fight continue. Our fighter continues to hit our opponent at will. The television commentators said that our fighter was not able to overcome the onslaught he received in the previous rounds. They said our fighter would not last another round. After seeing our fighter turn the tides in this fight, the commentators remain doubtful that our fighter can win.

This stage of the fight reminds me of a story in the Bible concerning the prophet Nehemiah. Nehemiah was given permission from his king to return to the city of Judah and rebuild the wall in ruins that surrounded the city of Judah. Once the word got out about Nehemiah and the wall, many doubters came forward and began to mock and ridicule Nehemiah for his effort into rebuilding the wall. People from all over helped in the reconstruction of this wall, and they made great progress.

Other "haters" heard of this wall project, and they became angry and began to furthermore ridicule Nehemiah. The "haters" plotted to attack Jerusalem in order to tear down the wall that was being rebuilt. Nehemiah heard that he was going to be attacked, so he staged men along the wall at various points to protect the wall. Many parts of the wall had large holes and gaps in it. These were weak areas in the wall, and they needed to be built up. There were volunteers who took turns working on the wall and providing security against attack. Some of them worked literally with a tool in one hand and a weapon in the other. The wall was eventually repaired in fifty-two days. Due to Nehemiah's faithfulness to the Lord, he was eventually appointed governor of Judah. Nehemiah's "haters" heard about this, and they plotted to lure him outside the wall to assassinate him. The "haters" couldn't convince Nehemiah to come to them, so they sent in a false prophet to essentially cause Nehemiah to sin and tarnish his good name, but Nehemiah saw the "wolf in sheep's clothing" with the false prophet. Nehemiah fearlessly accomplished what the Lord sent him to do. The wall was completely repaired. With that success, the psychological tables were turned on the "haters."

The conclusion of this story boils down to this passage of Scripture. Nehemiah 6:15–16 (NIV) says, "So the wall was completed on the twenty-fifth of Elul, in fifty-two days. When all our enemies heard about this, all the surrounding nations were afraid and lost their self-confidence, because they realized that this work had been done with the help of our God."

Although Nehemiah was mocked and ridiculed for his vision on rebuilding the wall, he continued to follow God's instructions to build. His "haters" were humiliated because the wall had been completely repaired despite their attempts to foil Nehemiah's plan. The "haters" finally realized that only God was able to facilitate the conditions in order for Nehemiah to finish building the wall. Although Nehemiah was ridiculed, insulted, and became the victim of a murder plot, he kept building the wall.

When people attempt to discourage and throw doubts on your dreams, just keep building and stay on the wall. When people talk about you and gossip behind your back, just keep building and stay on the wall. When Satan attacks your body with sickness, keep on building and stay on the wall. When your children fall astray and make the wrong choices, you better keep building and stay on the wall. Keep building and stay on the wall just as Nehemiah did. Do not get off of the wall and come down to the level of the "haters," you keep building on that wall. The Lord will provide for your every need, just continue to build and stay on that wall.

Just as Nehemiah proved the "haters" to be wrong, our fighter is proving the fight commentators to be wrong in their doubtful commentary of him. Our fighter attacks the opponent with hard combinations to the head and body. Our opponent manages to counter-punch and land a hard uppercut to our fighter, causing his legs to wobble. The opponent sees that he hurt our fighter and gets a sudden burst of energy. Our fighter is being attacked with both hands of the opponent. Our opponent has exploded with some vicious combinations on our fighter, putting him on the defensive, and he is trying to avoid this barrage of bombs that are being unleashed on him.

In the spiritual sense, Satan can drop bombs on us only if God lets down the protection he has around us, which may cause us hardships. Our most gracious and merciful God does not let us suffer for no apparent reason. His perfect plan for us is designed to draw us closer to him, even in our sufferings. John 16:33 (NIV) says, "Have told you these things, so that in me you may have peace. In this world you will have trouble. But take heart! I have overcome the world." This verse confirms that we will suffer in this life, but in him, you will have peace.

Our opponent looks to steal the round, as he puts his veteran tactics and skills to use. He slips punches well, making our fighter look a half step behind. With fifteen seconds to go, our opponent goes southpaw, freezes our fighter with a feint, and then blasts him with a left uppercut for a knockdown. Our fighter's glove touches the canvas as he tries to stay up and a standing eight is administered. Our fighter is dazed and tried to hold our opponent but can't find him. The opponent steps to the side and blasts our fighter with a one, two to the side of the head. Our fighter steps back and our opponent begins to attack. Just as our opponent steps closer, our fighter launches a monster straight right hand and catches our opponent on the chin, putting him down on the mat. The referee starts counting, "One, two, three!" Our opponent stands up, and our fighter is in attack mode. The bell rings to end the round, and our fighter is unable to follow up on the damage he has caused our opponent.

Our fighter is on a roller coaster of punishment. Whenever he makes progress, his opponent comes back. The television commentators write our fighter off, but his determination keeps him in the fight.

As believers in *this twelve-round fight we call life*, you must always know that God is with you. When others abandon you, doubt your dreams, and try to discourage your visions, do your thing and *stay on the wall*. I dedicate this chapter to Captain Thornton from the Provider Chapel. Thank you, sir.

LUSTS AND TRIALS

Our fighter seems to have caught his second wind, judging from his energy at the end of the last round. Also, he looked enthused as he sat in the corner. Our fighter looked across the ring and saw the ring girl wearing a bikini and high heels, carrying the ring card. The ring girl makes eye contact with our fighter, and she smiles at him. At this moment, our fighter is distracted by the ring girl, and he is looking at her in a lustful way. Our fighter has briefly tuned out his coach due to the woman he is lusting after.

James 1:15 (NIV) says, "Then, after desire has conceived, it gives birth to sin; and sin, when it is full-grown, gives birth to death." It is wrong to lust after anything, whether it is a person or an object. When you lust after someone, they become an object, and the object turns into an idol. An idol is anything you put as a higher priority than God. *Webster's Dictionary* defines lust as "intense or unbridled sexual desire; an intense longing." Lusting after another person is a violation of the seventh commandment, "Thou shalt not commit adultery." When you look at another person with lust, you have committed adultery in your heart. Lusting after someone is just as sinful as committing the act of adultery. Job 31:11–12 (NIV) says about adultery, "For that would have been shameful, a sin to be judged. It is a fire that burns to Destruction; it would have uprooted my harvest."

Lust promotes possession and greed; it is self-serving and self-destructive. We must live a holy life to resist the elements of lust. Romans 6:19 (NIV) says, "I put this in human terms because you are weak in your natural selves. Just as you used to offer the parts of your body in slavery to impurity and to ever-increasing wickedness, so now offer them in slavery to righteousness leading to holiness." In other words, we are weak. Just like we offered our bodies to impurity, we now need to offer our bodies to righteousness, which leads to holiness.

Another level of lust is when you desire someone or something so much that it becomes an idol. There are many forms of idols, and many people do not realize they idolize some things. Exodus 20:3 (NIV) says, "You shall have no other gods before me." Verse 5 says, "You shall not bow down to them or worship them; for I, the LORD your God, am a jealous God, punishing the children for the sin of the fathers to the third and fourth generation of those who hate me." This is not the type of *jealous* we think of. God does not envy us because we drive a nice care or live in a big house. He owns everything we have. He refers to *jealous* as giving something away to someone else when it is only meant for him. If a husband sees his wife flirting with another man, the husband has a right to be jealous because the flirt his wife is giving belongs to the husband and no one else. When we put something on a pedestal higher than God, then we are giving away something that should only be given to God. When we get absorbed in our careers and strive for promotions and positions to the point where God is forgotten, then we have created an idol in our heart.

Ezekiel 14:3(NIV) says, "Son of man, these men have set up idols in their hearts and put wicked stumbling blocks before their faces. Should I let them inquire of me at all?" A person may see their job status or abilities as something they look to more than the God who provided them with it. Some people get consumed with themselves, believing they achieved their successes all by themselves. First John 5:21 (NIV) says, "Dear children, keep yourselves from idols."

The bell rings to begin round eight, and our fighter goes into the round not fully engaged in the fight. His thoughts about the ring girl deflect his focus on the fight. Our fighter doesn't have the same intensity as previous rounds, and it shows in his performance. He seems to have lost the hunger to win the fight. The opponent is connecting punches that should never hit our fighter. It appears that our fighter has lost the desire and courage to continue the fight.

Deuteronomy 31:6 (NIV) says, "Be strong and courageous. Do not be afraid or terrified because of them, for the LORD your God goes with you; he will never leave you nor forsake you."

Satan wants you to fear any challenge you face because he wants you to fail. Satan knows that following Christ gives victory, so he puts fear, distraction, doubt, discouragement, and any other element of evil in your way to prevent success in the Lord. If you are mindful and recognize the times when Satan is messing with you, begin to pray, and stay in that realm because your strength will increase as you give your burdens to Christ.

James 1:2–4 (NIV) says, "Consider it pure joy, my brothers, whenever you face trials of many kinds, because you know that the testing of your faith develops perseverance. Perseverance must finish its work so that you may be mature and complete, not lacking anything." God uses trials to develop you and I, so that we can live the lives he intended for us.

Let's get back to the boxing match. Our fighter is trying to get away from the aggressive opponent, who is cutting off the ring. Our fighter tries to initiate clinches because he is off of his game in this round and he is tired of being hit. A straight right hand to the opponent's head gives a pause in the action and enables our fighter time to get on his bicycle and try to stick and move. Our opponent pursues quickly and is getting popped with jabs as our fighter starts to give angles to our opponent. The opponent continues after our fighter, missing with a pair of wild rights. Both fighters miss with a series of wild punches. Our fighter leads with a jab before landing a hard right to the head. Our fighter jabs and has our opponent up against the ropes. The fighters are in a clinch in the corner. Both missed with jabs. Our fighter lands a hard hook and follows with a right to the head. Our fighter then lands a hard right to the jaw and two uppercuts as our opponent's legs appear wobbly. Our fighter connects with another hard right to the jaw. A sharp uppercut by our fighter sends the opponent down on the canvas with sixteen seconds left in the round. Our opponent gets up at the count of "eight" but looks unstable. Our fighter starts to throw bombs as the opponent covers up and retreats. Our fighter is not able to finish our opponent off before the end of the round.

There were several lessons learned by our fighter in this round. First, a minor distraction, lusting at the ring girl, paid a heavy penalty for our fighter because he was not focused on the fight. Psalm 19:14 (NIV) says, "May the words of my mouth and the meditation of my heart be pleasing in your sight, O LORD, my Rock and my Redeemer." The psalmist asks that his words and thoughts be equal. Words of the mouth are a sham if they are not backed up by meditation of the heart. We all know people who do not mean what they say.

There was a point where our fighter lacked in courage and heart, but he gained strength at the crunch time. Joshua 1:6 (NIV) says about courage, "Be strong and courageous, because you will lead these people to inherit the land I swore to their forefathers to give them."

Our fighter went through some trials during this round as he contended with some issues of the heart and flesh, but he finished strong.

Acts 14:22 (NIV) says, "…strengthening the disciples and encouraging them to remain true to the faith. 'We must go through many hardships to enter the kingdom of God,' they said." You can expect hard times along the way, but God wants you to look to him for comfort.

Isaiah 12:1 (NIV) says, "In that day you will say: "I will praise you, O LORD. Although you were angry with me, your anger has turned away and you have comforted me."

The eighth round of *this twelve-round fight we*

call life has been turbulent, yet a blessing. Matthew 10:18–21 (NIV) says:

> On my account you will be brought before governors and kings as witnesses to them and to the Gentiles. But when they arrest you, do not worry about what to say or how to say it. At that time you will be given what to say, for it will not be you speaking, but the Spirit of your Father speaking through you.

> Brother will betray brother to death, and a father his child; children will rebel against their parents and have them put to death.

Blessings will always come out of hardships as long as you believe.

OPEN DOORS

Our fighter finished the last round strong, and he intends to continue this momentum. Our opponent seems to keep his hands low after he throws a punch and our fighter picked up on that. Our opponent attempts to throw a jab and misses, and our fighter comes over the top with an overhand right to the side of his head, causing his head to swiftly turn the other direction. With every punch our opponent throws, our fighter effectively counter punches because of the wide openings that are available. Our fighter sees these open opportunities and continues to take them. The referee steps in and warns our fighter about throwing low blows, but there is no low blow. They are good body shots. This upset our fighter who is focused on winning the fight. The referee warns our fighter about low blows again, but there was no low blow. It seems as though the referee is giving false warnings in order to buy time for our opponent to recover the beating he is taking. It is obvious that our fighter has two adversaries in the ring, our opponent and the referee. The referee has conspired to have our fighter defeated. Genesis 37:18 (NIV) says, "But they saw him in the distance, and before he reached them, they plotted to kill him."

Our opponent's team has planned to fight dirty from the very beginning and leave our fighter with no chance to win. God can make a way when there is no way.

It says in 1 Corinthians 16:9 (NIV), "Because a great door for effective work has opened to me, and there are many who oppose me." Just like our fighter took the openings of his opponent's low hand, God will open doors for us. At the same time, the adversary in the fight situation is the opponent and referee. If our fighter didn't take the openings, our opponent would eventually realize his hands were low and would raise them back up. God will open doors for us that we sometimes do not see, and he can close those same doors if we do not take them. Taking the open door that God opened for you will produce opportunities you never dreamed of, but it will also bring adversaries. The nay-sayers, pessimists, doubters, and haters will be there in an attempt to derail your train of victory. These people want you to fail, but it says in 1 Corinthians 15:57 (NIV), "But thanks be to God! He gives us the victory through our Lord Jesus Christ." Let the negative people be an encouragement to your victory, and use them as your footstool. Psalm 110:1 (NIV), "The LORD says to my Lord: 'Sit at my right hand until I make your enemies a footstool for your feet.'"

The below scripture is also a good reference when confronted with adversaries. Matthew 5:11–12 (NIV) says, "Blessed are you when people insult you, persecute you and falsely say all kinds of evil against you because of me. Rejoice and be glad, because great is your reward in heaven, for in the same way they persecuted the prophets who were before you."

Our fighter feels like he is being cheated and feels like he needs to do the same dirty tricks as his opponent, so he tries to get away with throwing kidney punches, which are illegal. Our fighter puts into his own mind that the opponent has the upper hand because he is fighting dirty, so he feels he needs to do the same. The kidney punches were getting through, and the referee did not see them. Our fighter started committing these little violations in the fight hoping not to get caught.

We Christians sometimes commit little sins, hoping not to get caught. Whether it's a little sin or a big sin, it's still sin. Concerning those "little" sins, Hebrews 12:1 (NIV) says, "Therefore, since we are surrounded by such a great cloud of witnesses, let us throw off everything that hinders and the sin that so easily entangles, and let us run with perseverance the race marked out for us." Little sins will hinder our feet as we run that race for the Lord. Those little sins will hold us from the blessings God has promised us. We must be mindful of those little sins we commit because that can be the reason our blessings are being held back. Anger, lust, gossip, unforgiving spirits, these sins are still sins.

Those little violations eventually turn into big violations because you will begin to believe you can get away with more. Satan, the ruler of this world, will plant ideas in your mind and can have you believe that the small sins don't count, and God allows you to do what feels good at the moment. The Ten Commandments applied in the days of Moses, and they are just as applicable today.

The conscience of our fighter got the best of him in getting away with the kidney punches. Our fighter knew the kidney punches were wrong, and his spirit enabled him to stop committing this violation. It says in 2 Corinthians 5:11 (NIV), "Since, then, we know what it is to fear the Lord, we try to persuade men. What we are is plain to God, and I hope it is also plain to your conscience." Our conscience is to our spirit like nerve endings are to our body. If we feel intense heat next to our skin, our pain receptors will give us the feeling of pain, which lets us know that something is wrong. If we commit a wrongful act against another person, our conscience will cause pain in our spirit, letting us know we did something wrong. This is conviction.

Webster's Dictionary defines conviction as: "The act of convicting; the act of proving, finding, or adjudging, guilty of an offense." This is what your conscience does to your spirit when you do something wrong. Proverbs 23:7 (NIV) says, "For he is the kind of man who is always thinking about the cost. 'Eat and drink,' he says to you, but his heart is not with you."

The manner in how you think of yourselves will be the limit of your potential. If you think of yourself as depraved, you will do reprehensible things. If you think of yourself as average, you will be limited to average potential. If you think of yourself as a champion, then you will do victorious things. In order to change your life, you must change what your life is centered on. You must center on that our God wants you to be a success, and all you have to do is believe. You don't need anything else if God is on your side. Romans 8:31 (NIV) says, "What, then, shall we say in response to this? If God is for us, who can be against us?"

It doesn't matter who is scheming to cause you harm and prevent your blessings, God will take care of those people; you continue to press forward in the will of God. In reference to those who scheme against you, Psalm 37:1–2 (NIV) says, "Do not fret because of evil men or be envious of those who do wrong; for like the grass they will soon wither, like green plants they will soon die away." Their day will come. As the old saying goes, "What goes around comes around."

The boxing match continues, and our fighter makes the right decision to fight without intentionally breaking the rules. Our opponent unloads four hard jabs to our fighter's head, but our fighter shakes it off and his nose begins to bleed. Our fighter throws some solid hits that are blocked, thus slightly disappointing our fighter. Our opponent counters the blocked punches with a short uppercut to the solar plexus, knocking the wind out of our fighter. Our fighter steps back to avoid further punishment because he cannot breathe. Our opponent sees that body shot hurt our fighter, and he tries to finish our fighter off. A couple more hard shots to the ribs and liver cause our fighter to go down to his knees.

There are times when Satan will hit Christians with body shots of sin, causing us to fall to our knees. You know, those times we start clubbing again, and we engage in all the activities that feel good to the flesh. Or you drive by the "crack house" you used to frequent and feel that craving to get high. Or you see that old boyfriend or girlfriend who wants to "hook up," and you've been celibate for a year. These are times when Satan has you down on your knees in your situation. Since you're already down on your knees, use those circumstances to glorify God and pray. I speak figuratively when I say Satan has you on your knees, but those are times when you literally need to get on your knees and pray for strength and guidance. James 5:13 (NIV) says, "Is any one of you in trouble? He should pray. Is anyone happy? Let him sing songs of praise."

Also concerning prayer, Matthew 21:21–22 (NIV) says, "Jesus replied, 'I tell you the truth, if you have faith and do not doubt, not only can you do what was done to the fig tree, but also you can say to this mountain, "Go, throw yourself into the sea," and it will be done. If you believe, you will receive whatever you ask for in prayer.'"

Prayer is how we communicate with God, not people. This is where we say what's in our hearts and minds. He is listening to every word you say.

Matthew 6:5–13 (NIV) says about prayer:

> And when you pray, do not be like the hypocrites, for they love to pray standing in the synagogues and on the street corners to be seen by men. I tell you the truth, they have received their reward in full. But when you pray, go into your room, close the door and pray to your Father, who is unseen. Then your Father, who sees what is done in secret, will reward you. And when you pray, do not keep on babbling like pagans, for they think they will be heard because of their many words. Do not be like them, for your Father knows what you need before you ask him.

> This, then, is how you should pray: "Our Father in heaven, hallowed be your name, your king-

dom come, your will be done on earth as it is in heaven. Give us today our daily bread. Forgive us our debts, as we also have forgiven our debtors. And lead us not into temptation, but deliver us from the evil one. For if you forgive men when they sin against you, your heavenly Father will also forgive you. But if you do not forgive men their sins, your Father will not forgive your sins."

Jesus does not criticize public prayer, he wants to denounce the self-gratifying motives that some people may have when they pray in public. These selfish motivations are designed to seek approval from people instead of God. Not all prayer is sanctioned by God. It says in Isaiah 59:1–2 (NIV), "Surely the arm of the LORD is not too short to save, nor his ear too dull to hear. But your iniquities have separated you from your God; your sins have hidden his face from you, so that he will not hear."

Our private prayers are designed to develop us. Our public prayers are designed to help develop others.

Intercessory prayer is recognizing the needs of others and bringing those needs to God. Do you ever wonder why you made it through a bad situation or your needs were met when you did not see a way? You can thank God for intercessory prayer.

As the boxing match continues, our fighter stands to his feet at the count of six and catches his breath. The fight resumes, and our opponent goes straight for the body again. Our fighter protects his mid-section, which leaves his head exposed to get hit. The opponent sees this and launches a left hook to the head and follows with a straight right hand. Our fighter does not budge and returns furious punches of his own. These two fighters are in the middle of the ring trading punches, fighting with all their heart. The crowd is on their feet, and the television commentators are screaming at the top of their lungs with excitement due to the intense action.

We all can go to a boxing match and cheer on the fighters with clapping of the hands, screaming and jumping up and down. If we can do that for mere human beings, then surely God deserves more than that. It says in Psalms 100:1–5 (NIV):

> Shout for joy to the LORD, all the earth. Worship the LORD with gladness; come before him with joyful songs. Know that the LORD is God. It is he who made us, and we are his we are his people, the sheep of his pasture. Enter his gates with thanksgiving and his courts with praise; give thanks to him and praise his name. For the LORD is good and his love endures forever; his faithfulness continues through all generations.

It is encouraged to jump and scream in the name of the Lord. Every time you clap your hands for Jesus, imagine that you're smackin' Satan upside the head.

This fight is a true test of will. Both fighters

continue to exchange blows with each other, but our opponent seems to have gotten the better of the exchanges. Our fighter is still in the fight but is behind on points. The bell rings to end this hard fought round.

In the ninth round of *this twelve-round fight we call life*, doors were opened and opportunities were taken. Adversaries took delight in attempting your downfall, and when Satan brought you to your knees, you used that opportunity to connect to God in prayer. God has made a way in turning lemons into lemonade.

ROUND 10

MONKEY BUSINESS

We are well into the fight and both fighters are fatigued and weary. They are both fighting with their all until the end. This is what makes great fights. Our fighter is working hard with the expectation to overcome and win this fight.

As children of God, we also should expect victory via Jesus Christ. Matthew 9:29 (NIV) says, "Then he touched their eyes and said, 'According to your faith will it be done to you.'"

Start living your life with the expectation of overcoming any challenge and trial you face. God will meet your every need in his due time.

The brawl resumes in the middle of the ring and our fighter appears to be weak in the legs. Our opponent is connecting with the same body shot to the liver and our fighter cannot stop it. It's clear these body shots are causing damage to our fighter. Our fighter scores a few punches, but our opponent is clearly building on his lead. About halfway through the round, the same liver shots are working against our fighter. Our opponent saw this body shot opening several rounds ago, but in this round he is able to set our fighter up to get this body shot off. Through the course of the fight, our fighter raised his right elbow whenever he threw a jab, and our opponent saw this and was finally able to set our fighter up to land a liver punch under the raised elbow. Our fighter does not know why he keeps getting hit with this liver punch. Our fighter thinks he is protecting his body with his elbows, but he isn't. Our fighter begins to wonder why he can't stop these punches from smashing into his mid-section. Our fighter never tried to fix this bad habit while training for the fight, and now he realizes that the uncontrollable raising his elbow is a weak spot in his defense. Our fighter has always done it this way and didn't know it was a serious flaw while his coach constantly reminded our fighter about this during training, but our fighter was convinced that he was not doing anything wrong and never corrected himself. Our fighter wishes he can change this because he is paying a price for making this almost uncontrollable mistake.

There is a scripture that I would like to reference the above scenario, as it says in John 5:1–9 (NIV):

> Some time later, Jesus went up to Jerusalem for a feast of the Jews. Now there is in Jerusalem near

the Sheep Gate a pool, which in Aramaic is called Bethesda and which is surrounded by five covered colonnades. Here a great number of disabled people used to lie—the blind, the lame, the paralyzed. One who was there had been an invalid for thirty-eight years. When Jesus saw him lying there and learned that he had been in this condition for a long time, he asked him, "Do you want to get well?"

"Sir," the invalid replied, "I have no one to help me into the pool when the water is stirred. While I am trying to get in, someone else goes down ahead of me."

Then Jesus said to him, "Get up! Pick up your mat and walk." At once the man was cured; he picked up his mat and walked. The day on which this took place was a Sabbath."

According to the above scripture, the paralyzed man came to the pool and relied on "man" to put him in the pool to be healed, but he was never placed in the pool. Man can help you in many ways, but man cannot change your condition. Only Jesus can change your condition. We sometimes blame others because we remain in the same conditions. Jesus told the paralyzed man to pick up his bed and walk. Jesus didn't tell the paralyzed man to get up and walk, he told him to pick up his bed and walk so to carry the bed with him. I believe Jesus told the paralyzed man to pick up his bed so the man will carry his afflictions to show what God has done for him. Never allow your condition to hinder your deliverance. Sometimes we are in a condition for so long that we say, "That's the way it is." Sometimes God will change your condition without you asking him because God knows you are ready to be changed.

Our fighter is in a similar situation to the paralyzed man because he has always fought in this manner where he raised his elbow and exposed his ribcage. Our fighter did not listen to his coach when he was told to keep his elbows down. Our fighter has a stubborn condition, and his coach is not able to change him from this. Man cannot change his conditions; only God can.

I want to mention a scientific experiment that involved five monkeys. A cage contained five monkeys, and a banana hung on a string from the top of the cage, with a set of stairs under the banana. A monkey would go to the stairs and start to climb toward the banana. As soon as he touched the stairs, all of the other monkeys were sprayed with cold water. After a while, another monkey made an attempt with the same result, and all the other monkeys were sprayed with cold water. After a while, the monkeys tried to prevent from getting sprayed.

The cold water was put away, and one monkey was removed from the cage and replaced it with a new one. The new monkey saw the banana and went to climb the stairs. To his surprise and horror, all the other monkeys attacked him. After another attempt and attack, the monkey knew that if he tried to climb the stairs he would be attacked.

They removed another one of the original five monkeys and replaced it with a new one. The newcomer went to the stairs and was attacked. The previous newcomer took part in the punishment with enthusiasm! Likewise, they replaced a third original monkey with a new one, then a fourth, then the fifth.

Every time the newest monkey took to the stairs, he was attacked. Most of the monkeys that were beating him had no idea why they were not permitted to climb the stairs or why they were participating in the beating of the newest monkey. After replacing all the original monkeys, none of the remaining monkeys had ever been sprayed with the cold water. Nevertheless, no monkey ever again approached the stairs to get the banana.

Why not? Because as far as they knew, that's the way it had always been done around there. And that's the way our fighter always fought, with his elbow raised, exposing his ribcage. I know this monkey story was lengthy, but the message is two fold. (1) It's all right to reassess areas in your life that have always been done a certain way. There may be a better way for you. (2) *Don't be a monkey!* God has an awesome purpose for your life, a life full of joy and purpose.

Our fighter is being "worked over" in the most savage manner, and it doesn't look very good for him at this moment. Although he is fighting back, our opponent is far too strong for our fighter. Our fighter is not backing down even though he is getting pummeled. This is the biggest fight of his life, and he is certainly standing firm in this battle. The only thing standing in between our fighter and the championship title is our opponent.

Christians must also go for the championship titles (figuratively speaking) and perform major works for God. Satan will always inflict distractions and provoke sinful elements your way. When you take a stance (boxing stance) in the name of Jesus, your shield of faith will diminish any cheap shot Satan will shoot at you. Ephesians 6:16 (NIV) says, "In addition to all this, take up the shield of faith, with which you can extinguish all the flaming arrows of the evil one."

Take that boxing stance and hold your ground against Satan and his ghouls. The more you resist Satan, the stronger you become. Think of it as resistance training in the weight room. Over time, lifting weights will increase your strength because of the resistance of the weights you are lifting. As you resist the vile Satan, your spiritual strength also increases. You can see as people lift weights in the gym, they have someone with them called a "spotter." The spotter encourages the person lifting to continue pushing through that set. The person who is lifting the weights is straining and breathing hard, but they continue to push with the spotter's encouragement. After the repetitions are complete, the person lifting is relieved and commended for their hard work through that set, and they have become a little bit stronger.

Christians have fellow believers to act as "spotters" when they bear heavy weights on their shoulders, and they need to resist the weighted temptations of Satan. We continue to push and resist these weights, in the expectation of deliverance and increased strength. When our set is finished with this spiritual weight training, we become stronger in Christ, and we can be an encouragement and blessing to others.

Our fighter is being picked apart by double jabs and hooks to the body. The occasional overhand right is making sure our guy is off kilter. Our opponent is winning the fight, so far. He's ahead on points without a doubt. He's the bigger man. "Our fighter is putting up a good fight but there's no question about who's winning the fight," the commentator explains at the beginning of round ten. The commentators ask each other if our fighter still has a chance to win the fight, and one replies, "Anybody has a chance! Listen, I always tell people that, in the sport of boxing, in the blink of an eye, the fight can change. Anyone can be beaten on any given day." This means it is not too late for our fighter to win.

It is not too late for any person to gain the victory that is promised to them through Jesus Christ. Although we get beaten and pounded throughout the course of our life, we can still have the victory. No matter how much you have sinned against God, it is not too late to repent and be forgiven. Committing blasphemy against the Holy Spirit is an unpardonable sin, thus leaving only one place to spend eternity. Matthew 12:31–32 (NIV) says about the unpardonable sin:

> And so I tell you, every sin and blasphemy will be forgiven men, but the blasphemy against the Spirit will not be forgiven. Anyone who speaks a word against the Son of Man will be forgiven, but anyone who speaks against the Holy Spirit will not be forgiven, either in this age or in the age to come.

Be encouraged that it is not too late to receive God's glory.

Our opponent delivers a flurry of hits to our fighter, causing the crowd to go ballistic, while our fighter tries to counter with a combination. "Again, our opponent is applying the pressure," says the commentator. A few solid hooks by our opponent leave our fighter's face looking awfully broken in. As the round comes to a close, our fighter is far behind in points, but he is still fighting like there is no tomorrow. Our fighter is aware that he needs a knock out to win this war, and he knows that it isn't over until it's over.

In the tenth round of *this twelve-round fight we call life*, we know that there is an expectation of results when we look to God. Psalm 5:3 (NIV) says, "In the morning, O LORD, you hear my voice; in the morning I lay my requests before you and wait in expectation."

We should look to God, and only God, for our provisions. "Man" cannot provide for you. God uses "man" as a resource for you, but God makes that resource. We know our spiritual resistance to Satan develops spiritual muscle which makes us stronger in Christ and better able to worship and bless others. The monkey experiment was somewhat humorous but effective in my understanding that it is all right to reevaluate our lives and determine if there can be a better way to improve our lives, according to the Scriptures.

ROUND 11

DO OR DIE

Round eleven involved some decent body shots and combinations, as well as double- and triple-hit combinations by our fighter, but nothing as damaging as he may have been looking for. "If he doesn't do anything with these next two rounds, then the opponent wins the fight," the commentator says. "It's the reach that's been giving our fighter trouble." One commentator asks the other why our fighter might not be able to secure a knockout. He replies, "You have punchers and then you have boxers. Our fighter is a boxer, not a major puncher, but if this guy was a puncher, it would be easier to knock the opponent out."

In our Christian walk of *this twelve-round fight we call life,* some rounds we get pounded, we get bruised, we get knocked down, but we always get up. We get exhausted; we lose courage and our desire to fight. God will not put you into anything that you cannot handle. God knows us better than we know ourselves.

This makes me think of Job and his life experience in dealing with Satan. Job was blameless and upright, one who feared God, and turned away from evil. Job was very wealthy and powerful. Job was considered the greatest of all men of the east.

The Lord and Satan had an agreement that the Lord will strip away the divine protections around Job, and show Satan that Job is faithful and will not curse the Lord during his times of temptation and suffering. Satan was given permission to work his evil on Job.

Job began to suffer with his animals being stolen and his servants were murdered by robbers. Then fire burned up his sheep and servants. Then his camels were stolen and his servants who oversaw the camels were murdered. To add fuel to the fire, his children were killed all at one time as a strong wind caused the house they were in to collapse on them. Though all this grief occurred in a short period of time and unexpectedly, Job did not curse the Lord. Job 1:20–22 (NIV) says:

> At this, Job got up and tore his robe and shaved his head. Then he fell to the ground in worship and said: "Naked I came from my mother's womb, and naked I will depart. The LORD gave and the LORD has taken away; may the name of the LORD

be praised." In all this, Job did not sin by charging God with wrongdoing.

Then God allowed Satan to attack Job's body because Job proved Satan wrong and continued to worship the Lord after Satan attacked his flocks and his children. Job 2:7–10 (NIV) says:

> So Satan went out from the presence of the LORD and afflicted Job with painful sores from the soles of his feet to the top of his head. Then Job took a piece of broken pottery and scraped himself with it as he sat among the ashes. His wife said to him, "Are you still holding on to your integrity? Curse God and die!" He replied, "You are talking like a foolish woman. Shall we accept good from God, and not trouble?" In all this, Job did not sin in what he said.

Job suffered to great extents at the hand of Satan. He was destitute and spat upon. Job never cursed the name of the Lord, but he did question him. In response to the Lord being questioned by Job, the Lord answered with a series of his own questions. The questions ranged from, Job 38:19 (NIV), "What is the way to the abode of light? And where does darkness reside?" to Job 38:33, where it says, "Do you know the laws of the heavens? Can you set up God's dominion over the earth?" Because Job had challenged God, God asked Job a multitude of questions that he was not able to answer. Job humbled himself before the Lord and repented. The Lord blessed Job with more than he ever had, due to his steadfastness in refusing to curse the name of the Lord. We must fight to remain focused on God because Satan will try to give you reasons to turn away from God.

Our opponent has become very frustrated because our fighter is still standing in spite of the abuse he is taking. Our fighter has a great determination and is in phenomenal condition. Our opponent sees that exposed liver shot and digs an uppercut deep into our fighter's rib cage, breaking a rib. Our fighter's adrenaline level has blocked out the pain of the broken rib, and he is returning punches with less force than our opponent. It's hard for our fighter to breath, and he loses some steam due to the lack of oxygen from not being able to breathe deeply. Our fighter feels in a state of bereave due to the pounding he is taking and not being able to breathe adequately.

It is inevitable that we will suffer and become sorrowful for various life reasons. Sickness, loss of jobs, divorce, and death can cause a person sorrow. Here in Iraq (this is where I am writing this book), I see fellow military members who are severely wounded or die from battle wounds, and my heart hurts tremendously. The Bible speaks of these issues in Matthew 5:4 (NIV), "Blessed are those who mourn, for they will be comforted." Bereavement can result from many avenues. I know that my God will comfort me in these times, and I pray the friends and families of these fallen warriors look toward God for their comfort.

Second Corinthians 1:3–4 (NIV) says about God's comfort, "Praise be to the God and Father of our Lord Jesus Christ, the Father of compassion and the God of all comfort, who comforts us in all our troubles, so that we can comfort those in any trouble with the comfort we ourselves have received from God." He is there for us in our most troubled times.

Our opponent opens with a left to the body, and then he lands a two-punch combination that brought the crowd to their feet. Our fighter comes back with a hard right hand that briefly halts our opponent's advance, but our opponent responds with a good flurry that shook up our fighter. Our opponent is all over our fighter, who is up against the ropes being hit with lefts and rights. He feels like he cannot go anywhere and begins to fear what is about to happen.

Sometimes Christians feel like they have nowhere to go, and their backs are up against the ropes with fear of what is about to happen. Psalm 34:4 (NIV) says, "I sought the LORD, and he answered me; he delivered me from all my fears."

Second Timothy 1:7 (NIV) says, "For God did not give us a spirit of timidity, but a spirit of power, of love and of self-discipline."

Fear is an element of Satan; God did not create the fearful spirit. Therefore, we should never fear anything but God. Fear of God is not the same as the human emotion of fear. To fear God means to stand in awe of him, recognizing your frailty and his majesty. It means to acknowledge him as your master, which requires a humble heart.

The fear that our fighter is experiencing, is the distressed emotion we all face from time to time, caused by the threat, real or imagined, of imminent danger. It is God's will that we should not be intimidated or have anxiety about anything. Philippians 4:6 (NIV) says, "Do not be anxious about anything, but in everything, by prayer and petition, with thanksgiving, present your requests to God."

Our fighter is up against the ropes and he is covered up taking devastating blows. He needs to get busy and get out of this dangerous situation. Our fighter attempts to pivot his way off the ropes, but he is pushed back and trapped in the corner. He is finding it hard to escape and cannot break free.

There are times when Christians may feel confined and in bondage to sin. John 8:31–33 (NIV) says:

> To the Jews who had believed him, Jesus said, "If you hold to my teaching, you are really my disciples. Then you will know the truth, and the truth will set you free." They answered him, "We are Abraham's descendants and have never been slaves of anyone. How can you say that we shall be set free?"

Do not let yourselves become a slave to sin. Believe that Jesus Christ can give you relief and set you free, and he will.

Everything our fighter does is ineffective, he does not know what else to do in order to win.

When you experience times of uncertainty, refer to Proverbs 3:5–6 (NIV), "Trust in the LORD with all your heart and lean not on your own understanding; in all your ways acknowledge him, and he will make your paths straight."

We cannot win this spiritual fight on our own; we need Jesus to fight our battles for us. The Bible says in Nehemiah 4:20 (NIV), "Wherever you hear the sound of the trumpet, join us there. Our God will fight for us!"

When you think he is not there with you, keep pushing through because he will always be there.

Our fighter is trying to figure out what to do with our opponent and win this fight.

James 1:5 (NIV) says, "If any of you lacks wisdom, he should ask God, who gives generously to all without finding fault, and it will be given to him." Many life situations leave us in a position where we do not know what to do. Instead of trying to figure it out for yourself, pray and ask God for the wisdom to lift you out of your situation. Don't leave it up to your abilities; give your problems to the Lord.

Thirty seconds left in the round, and our fighter needs to make something happen. All our fighter can think of is to start punching until he is stopped. Our fighter begins to unleash a barrage of punches on our opponent, connecting to his head. Our opponent stumbles backward, and our fighter advances toward him. Our fighter attempts to jump in with a left hook, and he is caught on the chin with a short right cross. Our fighter goes down to the canvas. Our fighter tries to stand but falls against the ropes. The referee counts to eight, and the bell rings to end the round. Our fighter is surely on a path to getting knocked out, but he is saved by the bell.

Our fighter is in a helpless situation about to be destroyed by our opponent, but the bell saves him. The prophet Daniel was in a helpless situation as he was thrown into the lions' den, where he was also saved by the "bell" of God. It says in Daniel 6:16 (NIV), "So the king gave the order, and they brought Daniel and threw him into the lions' den. The king said to Daniel, 'May your God, whom you serve continually, rescue you!'" Daniel was placed in a helpless situation, just like our fighter was placed in. But in verses 19–22, it says:

> At the first light of dawn, the king got up and hurried to the lions' den. When he came near the den, he called to Daniel in an anguished voice, "Daniel, servant of the living God, has your God, whom you serve continually, been able to rescue you from the lions?"
>
> Daniel answered, "O king, live forever! My God sent his angel, and he shut the mouths of the lions. They have not hurt me, because I was found innocent in his sight. Nor have I ever done any wrong before you, O king."

During the one-minute rest period, our fighter is restless, and he is struggling to breathe. Our fighter's coach says that he needs a knockout to win. He also tells him that he needs to go out there and fight the good fight and fight his heart out this last round.

In the spiritual realm, we must fight the good fight of faith, as stated in 1 Timothy 6:12 (NIV), "Fight the good fight of the faith. Take hold of the eternal life to which you were called when you made your good confession in the presence of many witnesses." We must keep the faith in the midst of our struggles and show others our strong determination in trusting Christ.

Our fighter's eye is swollen shut, and the other eye is half closed. Our fighter can barely see what is in front of him. The coach encourages him to fight regardless of his swollen eyes. The ice pack that is placed on our fighter's eyes reduced the swelling significantly, and our fighter is able to see everything clearly.

Mark 8:23–25 (NIV) says:

> He took the blind man by the hand and led him outside the village. When he had spit on the man's eyes and put his hands on him, Jesus asked, "Do you see anything?" He looked up and said, "I see people; they look like trees walking around." Once more Jesus put his hands on the man's eyes. Then his eyes were opened, his sight was restored, and he saw everything clearly.

This is a very important Scripture because this blind man, after Jesus spit on his eyes said that he saw men as trees. In other words, the blind man relied so heavily on "man" to do for him, that his mind saw other men much bigger than him. Jesus saw this and put his hands over his eyes again, and the blind man saw "man" as intended.

Our fighter's coach is inspiring for him to fight with every ounce of strength he has because this is the last round.

The eleventh round of *this twelve-round fight we call life* turned out to be a rough time for our fighter, who certainly suffered at the hands of our opponent. First Thessalonians 1:6 (NIV) says, "You became imitators of us and of the Lord; in spite of severe suffering, you welcomed the message with the joy given by the Holy Spirit." This scripture encourages us to joyfully worship in the midst of our problems.

Our fighter has rested, received instruction, and is revived to begin the final round of this twelve-round championship fight.

BUT BE OF GOOD CHEER; I HAVE OVERCOME THE WORLD

Our opponent is looking for the knockout in this final round, while our fighter keeps his hands close to block some hits. Our opponent lands hard jabs and hooks, at certain times making our fighter back up. Our fighter is thinking about all of the previous rounds where he was beat up and couldn't do anything about it. He regrets that he didn't do enough early in the fight. He begins to dwell on the past rounds and becomes disappointed to lose most of those earlier rounds.

There are times in our Christian life when we suffer hardships, we get bruised, and we can lose our desire to fight the good fight. There are times we get knocked down, but we always get up. We get disappointed, but we can overcome any adversity which confronts us. These past trials and tests already happened, and our purpose is to move forward and leave these former disappointments behind. It says in Philippians 3:13–14 (NIV), "Brothers, I do not consider myself yet to have taken hold of it. But one thing I do: Forgetting what is behind and straining toward what is ahead, I press on toward the goal to win the prize for which God has called me heavenward in Christ Jesus."

We must learn to get over the past and move on. From my experience, the biggest way to let go of the past is forgiveness. We have all been wronged by someone. Being wronged by someone is bad, but being wronged by someone you love is more hurtful. God commands us to forgive. Matthew 6:14–15 (NIV) says, "For if you forgive men when they sin against you, your heavenly Father will also forgive you. But if you do not forgive men their sins, your Father will not forgive your sins." When you choose to forgive those who wronged you, a release occurs in your heart and you become free of the weights that are holding you down and preventing you from moving forward in the plan God has for you. Start praying for those who wronged you. It can be a challenge, but press into praying for those people. We are commanded to forgive. If we want God to forgive us, then we must also forgive.

Some blood has appeared to flow from our fighter's right eye. Our fighter plods in, walking through screens of punches from our opponent. Our fighter is starting to feint with confidence and pick his punches. Our opponent steps in, but his short punches are most often deflected by our fighter's shoulders. The bout has increased in total punches thrown, and our fighter has the edge from the looks of this action. Our fighter, all of a sudden, looks very certain that it's his night; he instantly changes gears in his activity. II Chronicles 29:36 (NIV) says, "Hezekiah and all the people rejoiced at what God had brought about for his people, because it was done so quickly." God can make changes instantly. He can change your hard life into an easy life in an instant. He can change your employer into your employee. He can change your "haters" into your admirers. He can change your enemies into your friends. Anything is possible in the will of God. Philippians 4:13 (NIV) says, "I can do everything through him who gives me strength." Do not underestimate this scripture, because your breakthrough may depend on how you believe in the infinite power of God.

And to reinforce that we can do anything in God's will, it says in Luke 18:27 (NIV), "Jesus replied, 'What is impossible with men is possible with God.'" Do not limit yourself to what you can see with your eyes. Do not limit yourself to what society limits you to. Do not limit yourself to what your family or friends tell you. See with the vision that God has given you, and you will go places beyond any imagination.

Let's resume the fight. Our opponent looks very determined not to give up, but is decidedly uncertain as to how to turn the fight around, as our fighter is gaining some ground. Our fighter knows that he needs a knock out to win, and our opponent also knows this. Our opponent is not trying to mix it up; he just wants to cruise to victory. He doesn't want to take any unnecessary risks. He's trying to play it safe. This means our fighter needs to make a plan on how he will score the punches to knock this guy out.

Christians can lead lives that become bogged down with the everyday issues of life. These issues are Satan's way to distract you from focusing on God and sway us from our plans. The "hustle and bustle" of our modern culture prevents the meaningful items of the day from rising to the top. It doesn't matter if your distracters are financial or health related; they draw attention from the one whom deserves your fully undivided attention. The one who is most high and perfect. The creator of the universe. The one who came to earth and suffered the burden for our sins. The Lamb of God. Titus 2:13–14 (NIV) says, "While we wait for the blessed hope—the glorious appearing of our great God and Savior, Jesus Christ, who gave himself for us to redeem us from all wickedness and to purify for himself a people that are his very own, eager to do what is good."

We do not belong to ourselves, we belong to God. Mark 9:41 (NIV) says, "I tell you the truth, anyone who gives you a cup of water in my name because you belong to Christ will certainly not lose his reward."

God owns us because he created us. He did not sell us to Satan, we chose to run away from home and live somewhere else, but we are always welcome to return to our heavenly Father. He made us from scratch. It says in Genesis 2:7 (NIV), "The LORD God formed the man from the dust of the ground and breathed into his nostrils the breath of life, and the man became a living being." Here is some more info to prove he owns us. 1 Corinthians 6:19–20 (NIV) says "Do you not know that your body is a temple of the Holy Spirit, who is in you, whom you have received from God? You are not your own; you were bought at a price. Therefore honor God with your body."

Our bodies are temples and bought with the blood of Jesus, a very heavy price. Have you ever purchased an expensive toy for your child? I am sure that you made sure your child took care of that toy and did not abuse it. God purchased us, and he requires us to take care of our bodies because they are as a temple for Christ.

We are his pride and joy, the "apple of his eye." Zechariah 2:8 (NIV) says, "For this is what the LORD Almighty says: 'After he has honored me and has sent me against the nations that have plundered you—for whoever touches you touches the apple of his eye.'"

You are a very special person to our heavenly Father, and he wants you to know that. He knows this world is full of sin, but he cares enough to provide your needs and a way out of your disobedience. All you need to do is submit to him. James 4:7 (NIV) says, "Submit yourselves, then, to God. Resist the devil, and he will flee from you."

Back to the fight. Our opponent is tying up our fighter to burn time off the clock, and he is avoiding any action that can cause him to get hurt. Our fighter is now the aggressor, looking for the big knockout without any success. Our fighter is going to need a break real soon if he is going to win this fight. He needs to "steal" our opponent in order to get the knock out. When you hit someone by surprise, it is a term called "stealing" in boxing. The term "steal" means to set your opponent up for a punch that is a total surprise. It is usually preempted by a distraction such as a feint. You can also "steal" someone without a distraction if you have the lightning hand speed of Roy Jones, Jr.

There are times when Jesus wants to "steal" us because we don't want to do what God wants us to do. God looks to "steal" us when we are disobedient.

I want to tell a personal story on how I came to Christ. I was leery of all the hype about getting saved. I was in the world, and I had all the typical walls up so to prevent me from getting trapped in this Christianity. I attended a church service out of tradition, and an invitation to accept Christ was made by the preacher. All of a sudden, I felt the strong urge to get up and walk up front in the church. I couldn't resist anymore. These walls that I had up have been knocked down, and Jesus had "stolen" me. The same way God had stolen me, he can do the same for you. The Lord had "stolen" me on that one, and I thank him for it every day. The same way God "stole" me, he can do the same for you. It says in 1 Thessalonians 5:2 (NIV), "For you know very well that the day of the Lord will come like a thief in the night." God hit me before I knew it.

The boxing match continues, and our fighter lands some nice shots to the body. Our opponent is rocked by a combination and does a good job of tying our fighter up to avoid more punishment. Our opponent throws a couple of jabs and then ducks away. Our fighter can smell victory and he slips a jab and counters with a hook to the body and comes up to the head with another hook.

Just like our fighter smells victory, so do we Christians. It says in Psalm 44:7–8 (NIV) "But you give us victory over our enemies, you put our adversaries to shame. In God we make our boast all day long, and we will praise your name forever. Selah." God will give you the victory in trials. Be enthusiastic about his glory and majesty. Look to God as a child looks to their parents, with total dependence.

Our opponent's knees buckle and our fighter jumps on him with a flurry of hooks and uppercuts. Our fighter feels he is on the threshold of a knockout and feeds on that to get more energy. He feels that victory is knocking at his door.

Speaking of opening doors, Revelations 3:20 (NIV) joyfully says, "Here I am! I stand at the door and knock. If anyone hears my voice and opens the door, I will come in and eat with him, and he with me."

I am overjoyed when friends knock on my door to visit me. I am beyond overjoyed when I think about my Lord and Savior knocking on my door to sup with me. That is such an overwhelming comfort to know this."

The fighters pick up the pace and engage in a brief exchange in the middle of the ring. Our fighter complains about a low blow; the referee does nothing about it. Our fighter lands a nice combination, and the crowd starts with the chanting of our fighter's name. Our fighter unloads with an uppercut and right cross, causing blood to flow from the nose of our opponent. Our fighter unloads some big right hands, making this fight more competitive than expected. Our opponent realizes the truth that he is in big trouble and wants to distort what is really happening in the fight. He turns his head away, causing our fighter to hit him on the back of the head, which is an illegal punch. Our opponent complains about this, the referee gives our fighter a warning, and they continue to fight. Our opponent intentionally turned his head, causing himself to get hit in the back of the head. Our opponent turns his head away again, and our fighter is penalized for hitting the back of the head, with a point taken from the scorecards.

Our opponent distorts his complaint, and the referee falls for it. I want to mention on how some of the Holy Scriptures get distorted and overlooked. Do you know anyone who calls themselves a Christian but does not agree with everything in the Bible? You know, those people who believe abortion should be legal, but they know it reads as a sin in the Bible. Or the person who disagrees with what the Bible says on homosexuality. Their reasoning is because it is between two consenting adults in the privacy of their bedroom. What about the person who knows the Bible inside and out and quotes Scripture but does not live the way it instructs? How about the person who is hung up on and believing that different versions of the Bible interpret words incorrectly, and they read every other book in the world to prove their point, but they don't read the Bible? Do you know that person who is fixated on the name of God and Jesus as being the incorrect names for our heavenly Father and Savior, because they are not the Hebrew names?

The Hebrew names are acceptable to call on our heavenly Father and Savior, but God created all languages of the world, and the Bible does not prefer one language over the other. The word "ball" in Spanish is *bola*. In German it's *Kugel*. Whatever the language is, it means the same thing.

Revelations 22:18–19 (NIV) says about distorting the Word of God:

> I warn everyone who hears the words of the prophecy of this book: If anyone adds anything to them, God will add to him the plagues described in this book. And if anyone takes words away from this book of prophecy, God will take away from him his share in the tree of life and in the holy city, which are described in this book.

I pray this message sinks into the hearts of those who seek God's perfect word.

This fight is looking like what would have been expected. A knock down, drag out brawl. Our fighter manages to control the pace and our opponent is moving slower, but still dangerous, lacking in accuracy and not being able to hurt our fighter. This round sees lots of bombs being launched by our fighter and causing our opponent's corner to be worried. Our opponent lands a couple of power punches, but our fighter's retaliation is on the mark and damaging: It's an uppercut, hook combo and our opponent goes down. He gets up and gets back in the fight, but he's not steady. He falls forward one last time before again regaining his feet. This looks like the beginning of the end for our opponent.

We can also see the beginning of the end for Satan. Revelations 20:1–3 (NIV) says:

> And I saw an angel coming down out of heaven, having the key to the Abyss and holding in his hand a great chain. He seized the dragon, that ancient serpent, who is the devil, or Satan, and bound him for a thousand years. He threw him into the Abyss, and locked and sealed it over him, to keep him from deceiving the nations anymore until the thousand years were ended. After that, he must be set free for a short time.

Will our opponent be stopped tonight? He goes down again, and he still has a long round ahead of him. But again, he's up. He's not badly hurt, but he's taking a lot of punches. At this point in the fight, our fighter's action is blistering, and he continues to dig deep. At one minute to go, our opponent is refusing to give up as he is flailing away, and the crowd responds as our fighter answers the call. Our fighter is really showing a great level of versatility tonight. Our opponent is breaking down slowly but surely, but he is still able to cause harm to our fighter. Our fighter dominates the opponent for a period of time in this round, and the tides turn after a while in favor of our opponent. Our opponent briefly took control of the fight and caused more damage to our fighter for a few moments.

Just like our opponent briefly regained control in the fight, Satan will regain control for a short period of time. It says in Revelations 20:7–8 (NIV), "When the thousand years are over, Satan will be released from his prison and will go out to deceive the nations in the four corners of the earth—Gog and Magog—to gather them for battle. In number they are like the sand on the seashore."

Rugged and game, our opponent stays busy to the bitter end. Our fighter has sustained a gash in his lip, but he looks otherwise confident and comfortable. Always and again, it's our fighter's right hand that keeps finding its mark. Our opponent is not showing frustration or fear, but he has been losing ground in accuracy. In a final play, our opponent charges in and flurries. Our fighter is on the ropes for a moment, but when he fights his way off, he gets the good angle and shoots the "rocket" right hand straight for the chin, leaving our opponent hanging on the ropes unconscious for the count of ten.

First Corinthians 15:57 (NIV) says about Christian victory, "But thanks be to God! He gives us the victory through our Lord Jesus Christ."

Our fighter defeats the defiant opponent with a devastating punch that would have knocked anyone out. First John 5:4 (NIV) says for the Christian, "For everyone born of God overcomes the world. This is

THE FIGHT IS ALREADY FIXED

the victory that has overcome the world, even our faith."

Once the referee stops the fight, our fighter falls down to his knees and begins to worship God for the fortitude to sustain the agony and punishment of this grueling battle. During the course of this fight, our fighter learned to persevere through the agonizing times, knowing there is something greater for him in the end. This is true because our fighter is now the champion. The fans are cheering for our fighter, and he is thankful to God that he did not falter during those contentious moments in the fight.

Our fighter went through "hell" in order to win this fight, and the Christian will sometimes go through "hell" in *this twelve-round fight we call life*. Our fighter said a prayer before the fight, and he fell to his knees after his battle and worshiped God. Christians need to pray and keep praying. It says in 1 Thessalonians 5:16–18 (NIV), "Be joyful always; pray continually; give thanks in all circumstances, for this is God's will for you in Christ Jesus."

I started with this scripture, and I will finish with it to verify the end result, that we are victorious in Christ. Revelations 20:10 (NIV), "And the devil, who deceived them, was thrown into the lake of burning sulfur, where the beast and the false prophet had been thrown. They will be tormented day and night for ever and ever." This is where God knocked out Satan. This is the greatest knock out in the history of the universe. Greater than Marvelous Marvin Hagler knocking out Tommy Hearns. Greater than Roy Jones, Jr. knocking out Montel Griffin. Greater than Joe Louis knocking out Max Schmeling.

Our spiritual fight has already been fixed. Christ shed his blood for us so we do not have to. Always know that God is with you during every moment of your life, whether good or bad. Whenever Satan hits you on the chin, roll with the punch and praise God. This round emphasized the spirit of victory and encouragement, in the heat of difficult and arduous circumstances.

ENDNOTES

There are many religious leaders out there for us to choose from. So, how does Jesus differ from all others? This is like asking how the Atlantic Ocean compares to your local "fishing hole." There is no comparison. When we speak of Mohammad, he is dead. When we speak of Buddha, he is dead. When we speak of any other religious leader, they are buried six feet under, or trapped in a tomb unable to do anything for anybody. I am here to say that Jesus is alive! Revelations 1:18 says "I am the Living One; I was dead, and behold I am alive for ever and ever! And I hold the keys of death and Hades". There is no other religious leader but Jesus Christ who can make this claim and be truthful.

I am optimistic that this book has given some inspiration and insight into what is required for us to enter the gates of heaven. This is a spiritual warfare, and Satan is out for blood. The enemy is everywhere and has the ability to infiltrate every nook and cranny of your life, and he seeks to kill you. The good news is that Christ has already shed his blood and was killed on our behalf so that we can turn our burdens and battles over to him.

I have another personal story. When I was a child, I grew up as the youngest of five boys. My four big brothers "had my back," and I never worried about anyone messing with me. My big brothers made sure that they were the only ones who beat me up. Jesus is the same way, where you can depend only on him to "watch your back" and you are covered. Psalm 91:4 (NIV) says, "He will cover you with his feathers, and under his wings you will find refuge; his faithfulness will be your shield and rampart." He is your shelter in times of trouble. I love my brothers for protecting me, but Jesus will protect me in ways that my brothers couldn't.

You are reading this text because it was meant to be. God brought you to the text of this book for his divine purpose. You have been blessed to make it into another day, but tomorrow is not promised. Your life can end in the blink of an eye. It can all end at the next intersection you drive through, you never know. You may not know when it is your time to go, but you can know where you will go when you die. If you are waiting for the "right time" to go to church, now is the right time. If you are waiting to get your life together before attending church, think again. That's like saying that you will wait until you get over your sickness before you go see the doctor. God wants you to come as you are. It says is Matthew 9:13 (NIV), "I have not come to get those who think they are right with God to follow me. I have come to get sinners to follow me."

A Christian is one who has a personal relationship with Jesus Christ. That means we put our complete trust and faith in him. He knows everything about you and he loves you. He purposely sacrificed his own life for you. You are his prized possession. He looks out for your best interests.

If you have never accepted Christ as your personal Lord and Savior, there is no better time than now. Accepting Christ does not involve a major production of fireworks or running up and down the aisles of your church. You don't have to fall out on the floor or speak in tongues. All it entails is your personal trust and faith in Jesus Christ and that you believe he died for you on the cross. The salvation of your mother and father will not get you into heaven. You must make that commitment and choice for yourself.

No one is saved, based on their own achievements. You cannot be saved all because you are the Heavyweight Champion of the World. No one is saved because of their job title or community service. The only way to be saved is to personally accept Jesus Christ as your savior, and believe he died to save your soul. John 3:16 says it all.

If you would like to accept Christ as your personal savior, we can do this right now. It doesn't require an elaborate chapel with doves flying in the air and harps playing. All it takes is your humble heart to acknowledge him and believe that he died for your sins.

Read this prayer aloud and believe in your heart: "Dear Heavenly Father in the name of Jesus Christ,

I confess that I am a sinner and I have fallen short of your glory. Jesus Christ took the punishment which I so deserve, on my behalf, and through my faith in him, I am forgiven. I accept with open arms your offer of forgiveness and I place my trust in you for my salvation. I accept Jesus Christ as my personal savior. Thank you for your grace and mercy. In Jesus' name. Amen."

Your name is now written in the Book of Life. You called his name, and he answered. It says in Romans 10:13 (NIV), "Everyone who calls on the name of the Lord will be saved." Find a Bible-based church where you can worship and fellowship with other believers. I thank God for you, and I pray that you continue to do what God has called you to do. This is the first day of the rest of your life.

I pray blessings surround every reader of this text, and I declare in the name of Jesus that you are lifted in blessings in God's due time.

As a parting statement, I leave you something from Numbers 6:24–26 (NIV), "The LORD bless thee, and keep thee: The LORD make his face shine upon thee, and be gracious unto thee: The LORD lift up his countenance upon thee, and give thee peace."

BIBLIOGRAPHY

Bible quotation resource: www.Biblegateway.com

All scripture quotes from NIV Bible

Webster's Dictionary used for definitions

Book Website: http://thefight.tatepublishing.net

Book email: TheFightIsAlreadyFixed@gmail.com